ENDORSEMENTS

"What a privilege to read *Unbreakable Spirit* and to hear from no less than 18 women whose spirits are unbroken... to learn how that happened for each utterly unique life of beauty. Each in their own way discovered for themselves that if there is any power in this universe, it's in you and me, and the trees. Nowhere else. It is What we are. And that is unbreakable. Contained in this beautiful collaboration of feminine blessing is the most urgent message for all of us... to stand in our own ground amidst all pleasure and pain. The Goddess lives... in us, as us."
~ Mark Whitwell, Author of *Yoga of Heart: The Healing Power of Intimate Connection* and *The Promise: A Soft Message for a Hard Time*

"In a time when so many of us feel estranged from one another and frightened by the pressing concerns of modern times, *Unbreakable Spirit: 18 Stories of Feminine Resilience, Blessings, and Renewal* is medicine for the heart and spirit. The stories contained in this volume speak to our shared humanity, testify to the power of our resilience, and straddle the sometimes-great divide between grit and grace that is the hallmark of conscious living. Read this book and savor the vulnerability, the strength, and the hope it provides. I recommend this offering wholeheartedly."
~ Christina Sell, Author of *Yoga from the Inside Out: Making Peace with Your Body Through Yoga* and *My Body is a Temple: Yoga as a Path to Wholeness*

"This book exceeds its promise. Not only does *Unbreakable Spirit* share 18 (profound, page-turning) stories of feminine resilience—it reminds each of us our Divine Feminine can transcend circumstances. I can't think of a better time for this book to show up in the world. The masculine may be ready to fight—but we'd be wise to ask any of these powerhouse women what to fight for, and to what end."
~ Kristoffer Carter, Founder and CEO of Epic Leadership, Author of *Permission to Glow—A Spiritual Guide to Epic Leadership*

"*Unbreakable Spirit* is woven from the threads of our human struggle for awakening and renewal, courageously written through the eyes and hearts of the soul. As the urgency of our times begs us to remember and embody the feminine wisdom of transformation, these tender and bold voices lead us through thresholds, terrific challenges, and seeming ruins to discover the power of our own healing depths.

Together in harmony, they sing a song of inspiration for brave explorers going beyond gender and changing women of all times and places who seek freedom, sovereignty, connection, and the compassionate love that is born from self-knowledge."
~ Mary Angelon Young, Author of *Under the Punnai Tree*, *The Art of Contemplation*, and *The Summer Country*

"*Unbreakable Spirit* is more than just a book—it's a powerful collective testimony to the strength, wisdom, and enduring light of women who have faced life's darkest storms and emerged transformed. Featuring the voices of 18 remarkable women, this anthology invites readers into a sacred circle of truth-telling, where pain is honored, healing is possible, and renewal is not only a hope but a living reality.

Each story in this collection stands on its own as a deeply personal journey, yet together, they form a chorus of resilience—a layered, nuanced exploration of what it means to live through heartbreak, illness, loss, betrayal, and uncertainty, and still choose life, love, and growth. These women do not shy away from the truth. They speak with courage and vulnerability, offering readers not only their wounds but the wisdom that came from walking through them.

What sets *Unbreakable Spirit* apart is its grounding in the feminine. The stories are rich with intuition, connection, and spiritual insight. They celebrate the often-invisible labor of emotional survival and inner transformation. Themes of blessing and renewal are woven throughout—sometimes subtle, sometimes radiant. These women don't just survive; they grow. Their stories are not only about what was lost, but what was gained: self-trust, purpose, and a deeper connection to the sacred within. *Unbreakable Spirit* is a celebration of the feminine soul—unshaken, unbroken, and gloriously alive."
~ Carol A. Lampman, Director of Integral Breath Therapy

"The 18 personal stories in *Unbreakable Spirit* offer empowering and relatable examples of resilience to all of us women. We don't have to go down the drain in a flood of stress and hopelessness when faced with daunting life challenges! They prove to us that by opening to intuition and receiving Grace in healing and creativity, we can thrive and live a life beyond our wildest dreams. These women give us hope that, as one author puts it, a crisis is "our opportunity to become someone more."
~ Erin Reese, Author of *Truth Seeker: A Spiritual Adventure of Love, Loss, and Liberation* and *The Adventures of Bindi Girl: Diving Deep into the Heart of India*

"As someone who values sacred connection, *Unbreakable Spirit* resonated deeply with me. These stories are a powerful reflection of the divine feminine and the strength found in vulnerability. This book is a beautiful reminder that healing is not meant to happen in isolation; it flourishes in community, in shared truth, and in the light we offer one another."
 ~ Lisa Michelle, Host of *Illuminated Recovery Podcast*

"The world needs feminine wisdom now more than ever, and in this timely book of women's stories of resilience, you'll find renewed hope, strength, and wisdom to guide you through the twists and turns of life's challenges. May we all remember our own power and ability to rise together, no matter the storms."
 ~ Karen Kinney, Award-winning Author of
 Doorways to Transformation: Everyday Wisdom for the Creative Soul

Unbreakable Spirit

18 Stories of Feminine Resilience, Blessings, and Renewal

Compiled By Laura Joan Cornell, PhD
Preface by Hyla LeAnn Hitchcox
Epilogue by Susun Weed

©2025 Laura Joan Cornell – All Rights Reserved
Unbreakable Spirit – 18 Stories of Feminine Resilience, Blessings, and Renewal.

All rights reserved. Printed in the United States of America.
First Printing July 2025

Ananda Press and Divine Feminine Yoga support the right to free expression and the value of copyright. The purpose of copyright is to encourage writers and artists to produce the creative works that enrich our culture. The scanning, uploading, and distribution of this book without permission is theft of the authors' intellectual properties. If you would like permission to use material from the book (other than for review purposes) please contact:
Support@LauraJoanCornell.com
Thank you for your support of the authors' rights.

eBook ISBN: 979-8-9992441-0-9
Paperback ISBN: 978-1-7333923-9-6
Ingram Spark ISBN: 979-8-9992441-1-6
Library of Congress Control Number: 2025913564

Cover Artwork: Aimee Tomczak
Cover Design: Spotlight Publishing House
Copy and Line Editor: Hyla LeAnn Hitchcox
Curator and Developmental Editor: Laura Joan Cornell
Layout Design: Marigold2K
Publisher: Ananda Press
100 Sedona St.
Sedona, AZ 86351
USA

www.divinefeminineyoga.com

ALSO BY THE AUTHOR

Moon Salutations:
Women's Journey Through Yoga to Healing, Power, and Peace

Awakening the Divine Feminine:
18 Stories of Healing, Inspiration, and Empowerment

Unleashing the Courageous Feminine:
13 Stories of Strength, Grace and Awakening Through Adversity

FORTHCOMING:
Story Medicine:
A Guided Journal and Coloring Book for Women

DEDICATION

To Julie, Hyla, my sister Diane,
And all the unbreakable women
who challenge me to grow.

Thank you!

TABLE OF CONTENTS

Dedication viii
Editor's Preface by Hyla LeAnn Hitchcox xiii
Introduction by Laura Joan Cornell xvii

INITIATION THROUGH ILLNESS
1. Healing from Cancer ~ One Breath at a Time
   Camila Macedo 3
2. Defying Cancer with Faith and Business: How
   I Survived Chemotherapy without Losing My Hair
   Suzanne N. Mouelle 19
3. The Heart of Healing ~
   A Cancer Journey of Transformation
   Neelam Ghuliani 33

SPIRITUAL AWAKENING AND INNER GRACE
4. Learning to Live Through the Eyes of My Soul
   Mara Schachter 51
5. A Little Grace On Life's Playground
   Shauntay L. Williams 65

MOTHERING THROUGH THE FIRE
6. Pain Was the Midwife, Spirit Was the Medicine:
   My Daughter, Suicide, Addiction, and
   the Birth of My Power
   Jaque Hanson 81
7. Towering Chiaroscuro
   Lorraine Manzo 97

**WISDOM FROM THE WOMB:
SACRED CHOICES OF MOTHERHOOD**

8. The Arrival: How My Son's Brief yet Powerful Visit Opened My Heart and Awakened the Divine Within
   Emilce P. Suarez-Lipton 111
9. Sacred Choices: Soulful Conversations on Incarnation
   Julie Norman 125

FROM DARKNESS TO RECOVERY

10. Protection of the Goddess ~ How My Soul Gifts Pulled Me Out of a Chasm of Grief and Shame
    Rachel Chase 141
11. My Sacred Rebellion ~ A Story of Loss, Light, and Legacy
    Michele Campbell 155

BURNOUT AND RECLAMATION

12. Stepping Away from the Ledge, Coming Home to My Self
    Aimee Tomczak 173
13. Reclaiming Sacred Radiance: A Healer's Journey from Burnout to Blessing
    Maureen P. Murphy 187
14. From Tears to Treasure
    By Catherine Smith Bass 201

CROSSING BORDERS: SOUL INITIATIONS ABROAD

15. Welcome and Good Luck: My Immersion and Awakening in Nigeria
    Debbie Klein 217
16. From Violation to Soul Initiation in the Sacred Valley of Peru
    Cheyenne Marie Wright 231

SPIRITUAL COURAGE AND CONVICTION
17. Am I Going to Hell?
    Annette Jacobson 249
18. Life in a Battlefield: The Birth of Story Medicine
    Laura Joan Cornell... 261

EPILOGUE
From Stars to Soil: Remembering Fifteen
    Susun Weed.. 277
Acknowledgements 283
About the Cover Artist... 285
About Divine Feminine Yoga and Ananda Press 287

Editor's Preface

So much of life is a dance between the magical and the mundane. Creating music, giving birth, facing illness, making art, attending the dying, dancing... and gathering in a circle of women to share our stories—writing down the truths infused with the very essence of who we are. That is magic itself.

Writing a book is a joy and a challenge, a mystery and a leap of faith—a fascinating journey of synchronicity.

In creating this book, I met virtually with each author to edit side by side, always with the intention to hone her voice and honor her story. These uniquely feminine, collaborative editing sessions never failed to give me goosebumps. We played, puzzled, polished—peeling back layers to find the right fit, the moment when the flow of soul-words clicked into place like a key turning smoothly in a lock. We read aloud and listened. We breathed. We edited one layer, only to see another emerge. We laughed and cried... and created something beautiful.

I am so grateful to have held space for each author's deeply personal story to emerge like a butterfly from its chrysalis.

It is not an easy process. Dynamic juggling and "going with the flow" are integral to creativity within a Divine Feminine framework. Perhaps it is more truthful to call it *flow-work*. You cannot easily frame something as strong and shifting as the powerful feminine spirit. We women have spent lifetimes breaking out of constraints—those "frames" that limit our movement, our thoughts, our creativity, and our joy. Patriarchal systems have told us we are not enough.

But we know better.

We are strongest together—supporting and nurturing each other's growth as women, mothers, grandmothers, authors, entrepreneurs, and simply as human beings learning lesson after lesson on this path of becoming.

When we allow other women to hold space for us as we draw our stories from the depths of our souls and send our creations into the world, it is powerful—and healing on many levels.

We discover the "Mama Bear" inside us and let her roar free. We soften and toughen. We learn and grow. We find new peace inside ourselves, and we stand fiercely for what matters, whether or not we have ever borne children.

As for me, I am an author and editor shaping words, and a mother raising my children fiercely yet tenderly. Neither is perfect—neither words nor children fit the frames laid out for them. I celebrate their uniqueness.

I honor my nearly grown offspring, respect their true selves, and stand with them through all their fumbling and stumbling. It doesn't matter who they love or what their pronouns are. I love them unconditionally.

As authors and readers, we may not always agree. Our stories are unique, yet we share so much in common. We listen to each other, hold space with open hearts, and heal and grow. Sometimes that frisson of goosebumps lets us know we've brushed the unseen Soul, that living thread of synchronicity. And in this liminal space, may our minds expand to embrace more possibilities of what it means to be human.

We are women writing our stories. We are catalysts for each other's growth. We will be challenged, but when we trust our hearts and intuition to shape the process, what emerges is often more beautiful than we ever imagined.

Laura is a powerful guide and catalyst who coaxes out the heart and soul of each woman's story. I am grateful to have read these stories as they came to life, and to have held space for each to emerge, shimmering and unbreakable.

May these stories of eighteen awakened, unleashed, and unbreakable women fly far on iridescent wings—and may they touch, open, and heal countless hearts across our fragile yet miraculous world.

~ Hyla LeAnn Hitchcox, June 2025
Co-Author, *Awakening the Divine Feminine*
Copy and Line Editor, *Awakening the Divine Feminine; Unleashing the Courageous Feminine; Unbreakable Spirit*

Introduction

As you hold this book in your hands, you are being invited into the embrace of a sacred circle—a circle woven story by story, breath by breath, by women who know what it means to be unbreakable.

This is the third offering in an emerging library of women's stories I have the deep privilege to gather and share. We began with *Awakening the Divine Feminine: 18 Stories of Healing, Inspiration, and Empowerment*, where the authors spoke of how some of their most difficult life experiences led to spiritual awakening and their current work. Then came *Unleashing the Courageous Feminine: 13 Stories of Strength, Grace, and Awakening Through Adversity*, where raw courage and grace shone through hardship.

With this book, *Unbreakable Spirit*, we offer the powerful affirmation that no matter the storm, a woman's spirit—tended with love, faith, and inner strength—can never be destroyed.

But this book is more than a collection of stories. It is my offering to the possibility that stories themselves can heal not only individuals but the communities that surround us.

For twenty years, I walked a pacifist path as a Quaker, wrestling with what it means to live nonviolently in a deeply divided world. To stand in the middle of conflict and trust the possibility of peace is to stand in the fire. It is to listen when it would be easier to criticize or retreat. It is to seek to build bridges when so many are burning them down.

Laura Joan Cornell

I have learned that organizations carry shadows, and the deepest shadow is always the founder's own. I see this in myself: the war zones that swirl in my mind and spirit, the lifelong tension between my yearning for unity and the divisions that arise ~ in families, communities, countries, and within our world. That is why I wrote a new chapter for this book, *Life in a Battlefield: The Birth of Story Medicine*, to share how I have responded to my own battles by choosing, again and again, to listen, to build bridges, and to stand for connection, however imperfectly.

I am not a pacifist because it is easy. Indeed, in any war, the pacifists are often attacked by both sides! Mahatma Gandhi was killed by a Hindu, one of his "own" religion, not a Muslim, supposedly from the "other" side. I choose nonviolent social action (with storytelling as my current method of choice) because I believe in justice, because I believe in the oneness of humanity, and because I long for connection more than anything else.

Some stories in this volume shine a light on the potent edge between life and death: three women here speak of their resilience during cancer journeys, drawing deeply on their unique forms of spiritual strength. Two others share how they faced despair so profound they considered ending their own lives—and how the spark within called them not to follow through.

One author shares how she listened to the voices of her unborn children to help her decide whether to bring them into a troubled household, touching on themes of birth choice and the miracle of profound inner listening. Another tells of narrowly escaping rape in the Sacred Valley of Peru, surviving by summoning her strength to trust in her deepest soul guidance. Another recounts a life-threatening bout of malaria in Nigeria and her unwavering choice to stay in the country to learn and to grow.

In a world already so divided, I don't want this book to be another battleground. I want it to be a bridge. Though every story is personal—and therefore political—I ask our authors, and myself, to try to reach beyond the language of left or right, and to speak from the soul. That is what builds peace. That is what heals.

I do not claim to have all the answers. I carry questions. I know our world is shifting fast, and I pray to stay rooted in love, soul, and reverence for every person's truth. Maybe this is one of the deepest spiritual calls of our time: to honor each other's paths, even as we honor our own.

May you, dear reader, see your own unbreakable spirit mirrored in these pages. May you remember that you are never alone in your pain or your strength. May these stories fortify your courage, soothe your tender heart, and remind you that truth spoken with love has the power to heal us all.

Welcome to this circle. Welcome to these stories. May they bless you as they have blessed us.

With love from Sedona, Arizona — June 2025

Laura Joan Cornell, PhD
Curator & Developmental Editor of this book

INITIATION THROUGH ILLNESS

Chapter 1

HEALING FROM CANCER ~ ONE BREATH AT A TIME

Camila Macedo

How do you *trust* when everything you thought you were doing right turns out to have not been enough?

You breathe...

Shhh... Silence...

With the intention to release fear, and trust life, I breathed. Even though I felt insecure about the future, I breathed. Despite feeling ashamed by the disease, I breathed.

With so much still unknown, I breathed.

The year I was diagnosed with breast cancer was simultaneously the worst year of my life ~ and an immense personal growth journey through deep attunement with my feelings and emotions.

I processed *everything* as it happened.
I cried... released... made peace... forgave....

Delving deep into my emotions and wounds through the breath was essential for my healing journey.

Breath saved me.

INHALE ~ BREATH AS A GIFT

Breath is the bridge between the conscious and unconscious minds, revealing the beliefs that we hold about ourselves and our lives.

The Breath dissolves unresolved emotions, clears away physical, mental and emotional blocks, and puts us in touch with our spirituality.

When we breathe with intention, our inner healer is activated, so we can heal on deeper and deeper levels.

No matter how unconquerable the challenges you face, and how hopeless the future may seem, there is *always* a way through. Even if you cannot see the light at the end of the tunnel, the Breath will help you see. Even if you cannot see the path ahead, the Breath will take you there.

It's a *gift* to be aware of the Power of your Breath.

EXHALE ~ WHO AM I?

Since my teens, I've always been very healthy. I've taken good care of my body, eaten healthy foods, exercised regularly, and consistently followed my interest in health in general.

I've been interested in spirituality since I was young. My mom was very spiritual, and I enjoyed going with her to explore spiritual places. We didn't have a religion, but we were curious about various religions and spiritual philosophies. I even had the discipline to teach myself how to meditate.

When I was seventeen, the stress and turmoil of my parents' divorce ~ and my mom's breast cancer ~ prompted me to go even deeper. I started searching for life's deeper meaning and my own sense of self. I remember telling my mom, "I want to know who I am." I explored the possibilities, trying everything from individual talk therapy to family constellations.

With a solid foundation of searching for meaning, I stayed in tune with my body, emotions, and spiritual life.

In 2003, I started teaching yoga. The breath practices of yoga always fascinated me. After many years of teaching, I began to explore and study Integral Breath Therapy (IBT) with Carol Lampman, both for myself and also to add a new skill to my toolbox.

Around two years before cancer, a dear friend inspired me to start learning about Jesus as a teacher and mentor. I developed a close relationship with Him, which reassured me that I am always loved and protected... and always have been.

I didn't know at the time, but now I'm sure I was getting prepared ~ physically, spiritually, emotionally ~ for the toughest year of my life. I was physically the strongest I have ever been. I was secure in my spirituality, and I was happy to have found an effective tool ~ Breathwork ~ for releasing what I needed to let go of and for replenishing my energy.

INHALE ~ WHAT'S WRONG?

I felt I knew myself well.

So, when, in my early forties, I began noticing a strong pain in my neck and numbness in the fingers of my right hand, I *knew* something wasn't quite "right." I started to wake up at night feeling unsettled. I was tuned in right away to these subtle changes in my body.

Being proactive, I sought out specialists: an orthopedic doctor, a physical therapist, a chiropractor, a rheumatologist, and more. I hoped they could help me, but even though I did my best to explain how I felt, none of them had answers.

I started thinking it was post-pandemic tension and stress. Now, looking back, I wonder if cancer was affecting my musculoskeletal and nervous systems.

Around this time, I turned forty-five and was due for a mammogram. But I didn't feel confident afterwards. The exam was rushed. I felt *in my heart* that it wasn't enough. So I kept searching for answers.

One day, in the shower, I heard a voice that I now know was my intuition: *"What if it's breast cancer?"*

I told my doctor I felt unsettled about the result and asked for another mammogram. During the second mammogram, the doctor told me, "You have a family history. You should get an MRI."

EXHALE ~ I'M GOING TO BE FINE

The day after the MRI, the doctor called. I was told to come back "first thing tomorrow" for *another* mammogram and ultrasound "to check on something."

The next morning, I was *so* tense. The silence in the exam room was intimidating. I was not brave enough to ask any questions. The technician was nervous. The doctor, who I had known for years, came in and examined the images for what seemed like an eternity. All I could hear was their breathing. When I finally found my voice, I asked the doctor if she was concerned.

"Yes. Yes, I am." I noticed she had tears in her eyes.

Despite her tears, her words were consoling, "Your mom is fine. You're going to be fine."

Still, I was devastated. I sensed that she knew it was cancer but couldn't tell me yet.

Biopsies were scheduled for one week later. During that week that felt like a year, I couldn't do yoga or meditate enough to control my nervous system. I *needed* to control my anxiety, so I called my teacher, Carol, for help.

Even before the diagnosis, we were doing private IBT sessions as part of my training, so I called her. "I really cannot function. Please help me." She supported me during the whole week until the biopsies.

INHALE ~ THIS HAS A PURPOSE

I got two biopsies, one in the ultrasound room, one in the mammogram room. As soon as the first biopsy started, I felt a hug from Jesus. I started crying, and He told me, "*This has a purpose.*"

The doctor, intending to calm me down, said, "Don't cry," unaware that I was actually having a *very special* spiritual moment.

"*If this has a purpose,*" I thought. "*What is the purpose? Why is this happening?*"

When I went to the other room for the second biopsy... it happened again. I was hugged and again I heard, "*This has a purpose.*" The tears flowed.

I felt that a long journey was about to begin....

EXHALE ~ WHAT NOW?

"This has a purpose." I hang on to this assurance like a life preserver for the whole year ahead.

I had to wait a week for the results. The doctor finally called me and verified my concern. "Yes, it's cancer."

The following day, I called Carol and humbly asked her, "Please help me navigate this. It's really scary."

The holidays were quickly approaching, and there I was, scared and frustrated, calling doctors and hearing, again and again, "She will only be here in January." Thankfully, I still managed to see two doctors in December.

At the first doctor visit, when I first was told that a mastectomy was a possibility, I immediately started crying. The traumatic memory of seeing my mom for the first time after her surgery instantly resurfaced. Thirty years prior, the norm was to just remove the breast without any reconstruction. It was painful to remember.

My tears just kept flowing as this disconcerting possibility sank in... *"What now?"*

I had too many questions and very few answers. The second doctor I saw decided I needed more biopsies. Ultimately, I was told I *did* need a mastectomy.

While I waited, I had one month of breathing, asking for help, and dealing with my *very nervous* nervous system.

It felt crazy, but the mastectomy was scheduled for Valentine's Day. I decided to see the bright side of this coincidence, and appreciated seeing the hospital staff wearing heart headbands and red and pink accessories. It was not an ordinary day. They had LOVE in their hearts that day for sure! Seeing their good mood, and hearing them sharing their plans for after work helped me relax before surgery.

INHALE ~ SHARING THE NEWS

When I was first diagnosed, I didn't want to tell anybody. In the beginning, I only told my husband, my brother, and Carol.

Telling people was hard for me. I felt shame. I needed to be ready for their reactions, and I wanted to be able to answer their questions, so I took my time.

The funny thing is... *I* needed to help *them* calm down. It's tough for people to hear this news.

EXHALE ~ THE MISSING LINK

For me, the most devastating and frightening thing was being told that I needed chemotherapy. I didn't know I would need chemo until after the surgery.

Since I had consistently taken excellent care of myself, my burning question was, "*What did I miss?*"

I realized then how *essential* it is to manage your emotions and stress, and to access and release trauma in order to heal. I knew I hadn't been fully addressing my emotions, and could do better, and I was humble and open to learning. Therefore, every time I felt angry, fearful, frustrated, scared, or just was a mess, I decided I would acknowledge those feelings, because not dealing well with my emotions contributed to my getting sick. So, I told myself, "*Since I'm taking this whole year for treatment, I will also dive deep into my feelings.*"

So, at every step along the way, whatever the feelings that surfaced, I called Carol. Frustration, anger, anxiety about chemo, fear of the unknown... I knew I could call her, and I knew she would say, "We need to breathe on that."

I decided to "breathe on" every little thing. Even when I just wanted clarity. I knew I needed to learn how to deal better with my stressful emotions, so I did this intensely for the whole year. I was ready to go deep, to see what was underneath. I reconnected to my breath every time I needed to feel better. *Every time*, for the whole year. Each session was dense inner work. Carol's guidance helped me keep the wind in my sails.

I began to see my situation as a personal growth opportunity. This awareness led me to go really deep into my story, examine my wounds, and also to revisit my childhood.

I realized that this deep healing was the *true* healing, and, for me, the missing link.

Integral Breath Therapy sessions always begin with setting an intention. A week before chemo started, the fear was unbearable. I went into my session with the intention to reconnect to my bravery. As I breathed, I saw a haunting image of myself. With words and cleansing breaths, I discovered I could replace that fearful image with a happy and healthy self-image. Even though the cancer journey was far from over, I left that session with the affirmation: "*I am whole and happy.*"

INHALE ~ A FULL PIGGY BANK

Then... chemotherapy. For three and a half months, every two weeks, totaling eight sessions. Each session was five hours long. Five hours of breathing, trying to be present, and praying, while enduring icing my hands and feet to prevent neuropathy. This was the worst part of the whole nightmare.

During treatment, I saw a doctor who told me, "You have a piggy bank full of "coins" you saved for this moment. You can go through this treatment and you're going to be fine. I'm sure you'll do fine."

It was a powerful reminder of how good it is to save for "just in case," because you never know when you will be in a challenging situation. What he meant was that I made healthy choices. Each time I cared for my whole being: mind, body, and soul, I saved another "coin."

Even with a full piggy bank, I had deep work to do.

Breathwork was the essential key to my healing journey. I remember a tearful session during chemo in which sounds came from the depths of my soul. I released *so much*. Within the session, I talked to my husband, daughter, and mom, and asked them how they were feeling. This became a conversation with my mom in which I asked her to show me how she managed to be so strong when she had cancer. Her answer was so important to hear at this point in my treatment. It was deeply inspiring to learn that she had *abundant* faith and an *infinite* love for life. She, too, had "coins" in her piggy bank: Faith and Love.

EXHALE ~ A DISCONCERTING DISEASE

Everything that I had previously heard from chemotherapy patients was about how hard it is. Honestly, though, it could have been much worse. My digestion was not the same, and I did lose ten pounds, but I never threw up. I never had to skip a chemo session. I stayed on schedule, boom, boom, boom, every two weeks, and I never had to spend the night in the hospital. It was worth it to have saved the "coins" over the years.

At the same time, going to the Cancer Center was tough. My own challenging experience, while seeing so many other people going through their own versions of the same thing... That's a very hard environment to be in.

Every time I was there, I looked at the floor while I walked, because I didn't want to make eye contact with anyone. I didn't want to see their reactions to how I looked; I didn't want to see them looking at me with pity. Even though I didn't feel bad about my bald head, skinny frame, and pale look, I knew that some people would find it disconcerting.

INHALE ~ HEALING MUSIC

But even in the middle of all this, music, magic, and synchronicity happened!!!

Some years ago, before I was a cancer patient, I saw a video on social media about a group called Brazilian Voices. They had an Arts and Healing program in which members would sing for people during chemotherapy. I auditioned and was accepted into that program during the pandemic, hoping to get a chance to sing for cancer patients. But, unsure when the hospitals would open again to visitors, I decided to postpone.

During chemo sessions, all I wanted to do was just *be*. Breathe. Meditate. No talk. I wanted to be in my body. On some chemo days, live musicians would come to sing, play the piano, or play violin. I realized I was on the receiving end of the program I had wanted to be a part of. What a beautiful synchronicity!

In those five-hour chemo sessions, music took me somewhere else, far away from the discomfort and uncertainty. It made the sessions feel more bearable and helped soothe my nervousness. Sometimes I cried as the music led me even deeper into my heart, into my feelings.

I think, for almost my whole life, I hadn't allowed myself to deeply and completely *feel*. But, from the beginning of this journey on, I had decided I *needed* to change and vowed that I would be open to *all* my emotions, however they arise and whatever they are.

I would love it if, maybe one day, I could sing for people during *their* chemo sessions, because now I *know* how essential music is for healing.

EXHALE ~ BELONGING TO DIFFERENT CULTURES

Going through medical treatment in the U.S. is very different from what I know. Medical professionals treat patients in a more detached way than what I am used to, probably due to fear of getting sued.

In Brazil, people are very warm, including in the medical field. Medical professionals have a softer approach, especially when you are going through a difficult journey. Doctors will even give you their cell phone number... and hugs!

My whole family was in Brazil, knowing that I was going through this in the U.S. with my husband and my twelve-year-old daughter.

INHALE: SAME STORY, SAME DESTINY

My challenge likely made my mom revisit her own trauma, which was really hard for her. She couldn't come from Brazil to take care of me, so she suffered watching me go through cancer from a distance. She could *see* what I was going through. I didn't want to cause her more pain, so we kept the conversation light when we saw each other on video calls. It was hard for *me* to see her suffering. It was hard for *her* to see me suffering.

There was a session during treatment in which an amazing vision emerged as I breathed... my heart was sewn to my mom's heart.

I was in awe! *"How is it even possible that the Breath can reveal such extraordinary images and insights?"*

My mom had lived through the same story three decades prior and survived. Her breast cancer at forty-three and mine at forty-five were two pieces of our stitched-together hearts, our shared story and our shared destiny.

EXHALE ~ HUMBLY ACCEPTING HELP

I intentionally allowed myself to take the whole year to be just about me. I gave myself permission to *just live* and *gently* revisit my whole life story.

I have always focused on taking care of everybody else. Although I am a natural caregiver, this was the time to set that aside.

My husband was amazing. Since I first was diagnosed, he went to *all* the doctors and chemo sessions with me. He was always with me. He made the whole difference for me. He was *always* optimistic. He was always helping me find solutions, research options, and make decisions. I never felt such love and support!

In moments like these, it's amazingly clear who is really there for you, not just for the celebrations, but also for medical visits. I found such relief in this realization: We *really* don't need many people... we just need the *right* ones ~ and we had the *best* friends and family members who navigated the stormy seas with us.

INHALE ~ CANCER AS HEALER

At some point in the cancer journey, I realized I missed my father's calls. I knew he could also be dealing with his own pain.

He lost his father when he was just twelve, and he may have had a fear of losing more people that he loved. So, I opened my heart to him, saying that I missed him, and he started calling me more often, which made me feel more *seen*. This was healing for me, and I hope that it was healing for him as well.

In one of my Breathwork sessions, I forgave my dad for not being there for my mom when she had breast cancer and needed him the most.

Cancer was also healing for my little family. My daughter and my husband used to argue a lot. My daughter was also going through a lot in her own life, and was emotionally distant. I could feel that it was really difficult for her to see my suffering on top of her own challenges, but I didn't have the energy to help her or mediate their disagreements, although I would have loved to. While I stayed home, focused on my healing, she and her dad went out and did things together, which brought more harmony to their relationship.

In another session, I told my family, "This is happening *for* us, not *to* us." I promised my daughter, within that session, that we would live the best life ever after the nightmare was over.

Having my husband's full support and love also brought healing to our marriage. We both gained a greater perspective on what really matters in life.

Cancer was an *invitation*. An invitation to learn more about who I truly am and who my people are. An invitation to gain clarity about what life is really about. An invitation to realize that even though I can't control everything, I have the strength to handle *anything*. I'm not talking about the strength of fighting, but the strength of *knowing* that I am a resilient, Unbreakable Spirit!

EXHALE ~ PURPOSE

So much healing and beauty emerged from this challenging time. Everything has a purpose indeed.

I learned *a lot more* about myself. I was reassured that through using the breath, healing my wounds and telling my story, I'm fulfilling my purpose with kindness and love ~ to inspire and guide women through their healing and transformation as they get in touch with their breath, body, and emotions.

All the inner work I've done, and my desire to help others to dive deep is because I believe we are here to *know ourselves, heal ourselves, transform our lives,* and to *awaken, evolve,* and *be in service...*

~ One breath at a time. ~

ABOUT CAMILA MACEDO

Born and raised in Brazil, Camila Macedo pursued a career in dentistry before her true passion for personal growth became the driving force of her life. At seventeen, Camila faced a significant turning point when her parents got divorced and her mom had breast cancer. This challenging period sparked her commitment to inner exploration and personal development.

Camila has been a devoted yoga teacher for over two decades, guiding countless individuals on their paths to balance and well-being. Her expertise has evolved, leading her to focus on Breathwork as a transformative tool. Breathwork, for Camila, is not just a technique but a gateway to self-discovery, stress management, and therapeutic healing.

In 2023, Camila's life took an unexpected turn when she was diagnosed with breast cancer.

Camila's approach to self-care, self-respect, and appreciation for life evolved profoundly due to this challenge. Her understanding of vulnerability and strength deepened, enriching her practice and perspective.

Camila is dedicated to supporting women over forty who are seeking support and guidance on their own paths to wellness, healing, transformation, and empowerment.

Instagram: @camilamacedo.healing

Email: camilamacedo.healing@gmail.com

For a free Breathwork exercise recording, please email me.

Chapter 2

DEFYING CANCER WITH FAITH AND BUSINESS:
HOW I SURVIVED CHEMOTHERAPY WITHOUT LOSING MY HAIR

Suzanne N. Mouelle, MBA

At first glance, business and brand building do not seem to have anything to do with the life of a person diagnosed with cancer and undergoing chemotherapy treatment. Yet, in fact, in my story, it does....

When I was diagnosed with blood cancer (lymphoma), I was told that the required treatment I needed was not available in my home country of Cameroon. At that time, I was making a good living in a thriving Business Management career as a Brand Marketing Corporate Professional.

A cancer diagnosis was the last thing I ever expected... because I was physically quite healthy, and I was living an emotionally and spiritually fulfilled lifestyle—happily married to a wonderful Man of God.

THE FIRST SYMPTOMS

I developed a cough that would not cease despite taking medication, and discovered swollen lymph nodes in my armpit which worried me to the point where, eventually, I was hospitalized.

"*What is this?*" I wondered... I thought it was a skin condition that would go away after applying some type of over-the-counter ointment. Unfortunately, the nodes did not disappear. Instead, I began finding more of them on my chest and neck, as if they were spreading, and I kept coughing even more, day and night.

Another unusual symptom that appeared was abundant sweating at night. I had to place a towel on top of my bed sheets to absorb it, and get up to change sheets up to three times in the same night.

THE FIRST WRONG DIAGNOSIS

When I was hospitalized for excessive coughing, the doctor who was caring for me made a wrong diagnosis, telling me that I was suffering from tuberculosis. I was very surprised and upset by his diagnosis. I contested it, because I knew that I was not living in the type of overcrowded environment that brings on that type of disease.

I challenged that wrong "verdict" and requested another set of exams to find out exactly what I was suffering from. I asked the medical team to do a biopsy in order to determine the cause of the inflamed lymph nodes scattered on my upper body.

In the meantime, my doctors administered heavy tuberculosis treatment for two months. It made me so weak I could no longer read nor write properly. I almost lost my mind.

THE REAL "BAD" NEWS

The news came two months later with the test results. I was diagnosed with Non-Hodgkin's lymphoma, a serious type of blood cancer. While discussing it, the oncologist asked me to select the country where I wanted to take the chemotherapy treatment, since there was no hospital properly equipped to take care of my case in Cameroon. Non-Hodgkin's lymphoma is the most frequently diagnosed blood cancer in Cameroon with a 31.1% prevalence. Unfortunately, poorly equipped medical facilities and lack of specialized personnel to administer the care, not to mention the fact that chemotherapy drugs were frequently out of stock due to their high cost, caused doctors to prescribe treatment abroad.[1]

When I got the news, I could hardly believe it. I kept asking myself, *"What happened? What did I do wrong? Was it a curse, a spell, a 'spiritual attack'?"* I resolved to treat the situation as an "enemy" that I would have to fight and overcome. I stayed quiet throughout the long drive back home, pondering how I would announce the news to my husband and close family.

I also began thinking about how I would organize my six-month sick leave from work. I had to prepare to travel to South Africa, which was the most affordable medical care offer and closest hospital location to my home country. I wondered how the whole situation would affect my life, my job and my overall future....

THE DECISION TO TRAVEL FOR CHEMOTHERAPY

As a fervent Christian, I believe in miracles! I had read many stories of Jesus healing the sick in the Bible-which to me is God's goodwill for my life. My husband is a full time Gospel Minister, and we both believe in the power of prayer according to God's word.

As a Minister's wife, I had witnessed many cases where people came to our home Church with critical health conditions that could not be resolved in hospitals. They received miraculous healing after prayer. I recall the case of a young woman who came in with a sickness that almost made her blind. She had blisters

---

[1] medicaltrip.com

on her face, including a couple on her left eye that caused her eyelids to close and threatened her vision. The local name for this condition is "Zona," better known as herpes zoster or shingles. It is not easily cured due to the high cost and unavailability of antiviral medication. After a month of prayers, she recovered her health and sight.

Seeing that, I could easily lean on the belief that the same God who had previously healed many people before me using my husband's "anointed" hands could heal me as well if he prayed for me. That is exactly what he was planning to do. In fact, my husband did not want to hear anything about my undergoing chemotherapy to heal the disease. He believed God could heal me miraculously, if we just prayed in one accord.

However, I wanted to make sure this was the perfect method for God to heal me. Although I had the same faith as my husband, I wanted the healing to happen God's way. So, in my prayers, I asked God how He wanted me to be healed: through prayer only, or through chemotherapy? After praying a few times, as I was sleeping soundly one night, I received my answer in a dream. I was walking alone in a dark corridor. I could hardly see what was around me. All of a sudden, I noticed that there was a large soldier in full armor (helmet, breastplate, sword, and shield) walking in front of me. It felt safe to follow him, and as I did, I saw that we were heading towards the end of the corridor where I could see a bright light beaming in. The dark corridor scene in my dream reminded me of how chemotherapy had been described to me: a harsh, scary and solitary journey that I would have to go through.

Nonetheless, I knew I was being escorted to my healing destination and that no matter how dark the upcoming days would be, I would make it through. This was the main sign I received indicating that God's WILL for me was to go through the chemotherapy journey. He later confirmed this with a Bible scripture I found in Psalms 23:4 (KJV)[2] ~ *"Even though I walk through the valley of the shadow of death, I fear no evil, for you are with me...."*

I shared the dream with my husband. We both agreed to go through this together and to combine scientific medical cure with faith and prayer. I was grateful for his support of my decision, since in both African culture and the Christian religion, wives are expected to submit to their husbands. Consequently, I went on to start chemotherapy treatment in Johannesburg, South Africa.

My Hair Story before Leaving

One of the first things the oncologist told me was that I would lose my hair as a result of the chemotherapy. Therefore, in order to avoid the shock of seeing my long hair fall off in one day on my bed, I went to my hairdresser and asked her to cut it all off as short as possible. This was a bold decision even my hairdresser was scared to execute, because of how long African hair takes to grow back.

As much as I was psychologically prepared to see my hair fall, I had no idea of the pain I was going to endure during the treatment. Thank God, before leaving, I ensured I had both my husband and my mentor's spiritual support. I knew that they were going to pray for me, and that no matter how bad my condition was, I would be okay.

The First Days of Treatment

Chemotherapy was very harsh in the beginning, because I didn't really know what to expect. It is a very daunting experience. I felt crushed after taking the first drip.

---

[2] King James Version

Thank God I was an outpatient, so I just went to the hospital to take the IV drips and after the various colored solutions were injected into my body, I would go back to my guest house room to rest. That is when the ordeal would start: I began feeling dizzy, completely weak, and nauseous, and had to take so many various drugs. I felt like I'd been run over by a truck, and I would spend most of my time sleeping during the first three days. My appearance, too, was changing in an alarming way: I was getting darker in complexion and my gloomy face was scary to many people around me. In fact, some of the women who were cleaning my room stopped coming because they were afraid to find me dead on my bed.

I had not noticed my change of appearance until I went on a short Christmas vacation back to my home country. When my husband saw me, he did not mention anything to me. However, when my spiritual mentor asked him how I was doing, he replied: "She is very dark and skinny." My spiritual mentor responded jokingly: "You've married a black woman. What did you expect?"

I loved the way everyone in my family and my church community was caring about me. Most of them did not know the trauma I was going through. All they knew was that I was sick. No one, except my very close family, knew that I was suffering from cancer. My husband and I had decided not to disclose the information to prevent our loved ones from being scared or panicking. Cancer is a very scary disease that takes the lives of many people in our country because most people cannot afford the treatment costs. Nonetheless, I felt a lot of love and empathy from my community, which enabled me to endure the challenges of the disease, especially when I was alone in my room, far from home.

Additionally, during my stay at the guesthouse, I met Cecilia, a very nice South African woman. She was one of the cleaners, and was kind enough to serve me breakfast in my room. She was my "feminine guardian angel." After her daily duties, she would come to visit me, massage my swollen arms, and help care for me. As we shared our personal stories ~ me visiting from a foreign country seeking a cure and her telling me about her tough living conditions in a shack ~ we got better acquainted. I encouraged her with my testimonies of hope, faith, and resilience and eventually became her spiritual mentor.

MY MIRACULOUS HAIR STORY

When I travelled to South Africa, I brought a little bottle of avocado oil I'd been using back home to moisturize my hair. Every night, I would apply it before tying my head with a scarf to sleep. I dreaded waking up and seeing all my hair gone, so every morning I fearfully untied my scarf expecting to see fallen hair in it. To my great surprise, three months into chemotherapy treatment, my hair did not fall out at all; instead, it was growing!

In one of my quiet times, as I was pondering about my uncommon and unpredicted situation, I received an answer in my heart telling me: "*I am your Creator. I am the One who made your body and your hair; it is counted, and no hair can fall from your scalp unless I allow it.*" At first, I was skeptical when I heard that gentle voice. However, it wasn't until I found the corresponding scriptures while reading the Bible that I realized it was coming from God. The confirming verses were stated as follows: "*The very hairs of your head are numbered.*" Luke 12:7 (KJV); "*Not a hair on your head shall perish.*" Luke 21:18 (NIV).[3]

I continued to apply avocado oil on my hair, and although it thinned, it never fell out. From that spiritual experience, I understood that my life was in God's hands. He was protecting me, and I would recover. Moreover, from my organic avocado oil hair experience, I realized that God has put solutions in nature that He has created, and we can use them to heal many of our

---

[3] New International Version

ailments. We can find cures in plants, fruits, vegetables, seeds, trees and many other natural resources.

This realization inspired my decision to develop a range of organic beauty and wellness products using natural ingredients from our local gardens. The plan of turning this idea into a business and a Legacy brand emerged. As a Brand Marketer, I started pursuing that goal.

THE BIRTH OF MY LEGACY BUSINESS BRAND

I started developing a new range of organic products as well as their packaging designs. Every time I did, I noticed I felt better physically, emotionally and mentally. The idea of seeing the products come to life made me very happy.

I had already started to develop a range of organic hand-made soaps and body oils, but I considered it a side hobby more than a real business. I was not yet ready to leave the comfort of my well-paying job to venture into the unknown and unpredictable field of entrepreneurship. It appeared that the disease had come to push me into my calling: Business Brand Building. That's how the *Natural Garden* brand was born.

Not only did this new activity keep me busy, it also made me realize how meaningful my life was. It convinced me that I should make the most out of life, leaving a Legacy to my daughter and my family. Launching my organic beauty and wellness business was the right avenue to achieve that goal. Coincidently, a former Packaging Designer I had worked with felt compelled to support me. She offered the opportunity of working with her creative design team to enhance my product packaging for FREE. This was another sign from heaven confirming that it was the right timing for the task. I accepted and welcomed her offer with great gratitude.

No matter how I felt, although it seemed like I was dying on the outside ~ with dull, darkened skin, ugly blackened nails, and weird-looking eyes as the result of the chemotherapy chemicals ~ I was experiencing a rebirth inside. My new activity enabled me to stay focused on positive outcomes, and keep my mind away from my physical ordeal. Working on my product packaging empowered me to fight the symptoms of the disease (dizziness, pain, weakness and feeling sleepy most of the time). I was awake, alert, creative, energetic, and excited. Every time I had strength, I was working on my craft. I attended meetings with the creative design team and planned the project's next steps. The mere idea of launching my brand gave me the desire to live my life to the fullest, and triggered my intention to leave a Legacy. I am proud to see the business grow to this day.

Conquering Fear

What is FEAR? I would define it as the **F**alse **E**vidence of an **A**ppearing **R**eality.

During my time going through chemotherapy, I discovered that fear is not just a feeling. It is a spiritual entity that comes to haunt people through their mind. It uses negative thoughts to ruin their emotions. It is a spiritual "wind" that steals your peace, your joy, your strength, your vision and your ambition.

In the Bible, it is described as a "spirit" that can be conquered by God's Spirit in us: *"For God has not given us a spirit of fear, but of power, love and self-discipline."* 2 Timothy 1:7 (NLT).[4] Based on that scripture, I believe we can discipline our minds to conquer fear, provided we are aware of the Spirit of God working within us.

---

[4] New Living Translation

Because I was motivated to live out my purpose, I was no longer victim to the chemotherapy and its emotional, mental, and physical challenges. I had welcomed my situation as the opportunity to fulfil my dream, using my "free time" to work on my product packaging. In my view, how we perceive our seemingly negative situations, and what we believe, has an impact on the outcome. Fear is the opposite of believing or having faith. Today, I am a witness that faith can influence our thinking pattern, even to the point where it overrides negative thoughts and enables us to conquer fear.

EMBRACING FAITH

What is FAITH? It is the **F**irm **A**ssurance **I**n the **T**ruth from **H**eaven. My definition is inspired by this verse: *"Faith is the substance of things hoped for, the evidence of things not seen."* Hebrews 11:1 (KJV).

Faith is the foundation of my story. I believe that God exists, He is alive, He loves me and He has my best interest at heart. He is the Creator of all things that I see: nature, the animals, the wind, the sun, the moon, and human beings. I believe He created me and He knows me better than anyone. When something goes wrong, He can fix it because He wants me to thrive, be happy, be healthy, be wealthy and live well. I have also accepted Jesus as my Lord and Saviour, which enables God's Spirit to flow in and through me.

Because of my belief, I applied my faith throughout the illness, the treatment and the healing journey. Faith is the main strategy I used to conquer all my fears including the fear of death, which typically comes when we receive a cancer diagnosis.

MY FAITH STRATEGIES TO OVERCOME FEAR

While reading the Bible during treatment, I collected all the scriptures in relation to God's promises of healing. I used to meditate on this particular one and declare it as my "power affirmation" ~ *"By His (Jesus') stripes I've been healed."* Isaiah: 53:5 (NKJV).[5] Therefore, I would often say to myself, *"I am healed!"*

Another strategy I remember is talking to my body before chemotherapy sessions at the hospital. While showering, I would speak words like these: *"My dear body, you are the temple of God, wonderfully made by Him. No matter what goes into you through the drips, it is not meant to harm you, but to cleanse you. Just like getting a team of pest control experts to fumigate my house to kill the pests, your job is to let the drips perform their cleansing duty, and to evacuate them as soon as they are done."* With that type of mindset, I would go into the chemotherapy session feeling strong, and come out of it knowing that I could overcome all the side effects, because they were temporary. Positive affirmations spoken to my body and the power of prayer played an essential role in my healing.

One last activity that helped me overcome the disease and dispel the fear of death from my mind was reading Bible scriptures and listening to preachers speaking the word of God. Every morning, after spending my personal time praying, reading and proclaiming "power affirmations" about the promises of healing found in the Bible, I would tune in and listen to Christian television programs. Doing that enabled me to focus on healthier outcomes, keep a positive attitude, and strengthen my faith.

This is the message I wanted to get across to you, dear reader. You can overcome cancer and any life-threatening situation by having the right mindset and a strong faith. With your real passion and your skills, you can develop a Legacy business, or a purpose-driven activity that will generate income and help you thrive in life.

---

[5] New King James Version

In the Bible, it is written: "*All things are possible to those who believe.*" Mark 9:23 (NIV), and "*Let it be done unto you according to your faith.*" Matthew 9:29 (CSB).[6] The question is: "*Do you believe?*" If yes, let it be done unto you, according to your faith. God bless you!

---

[6] Christian Standard Bible

ABOUT SUZANNE N. MOUELLE, MBA

Suzanne N. Mouelle, MBA is a seasoned Marketing Consultant, Brand Strategy Expert, and Packaging Specialist who helps Business Owners and Corporate Professionals transform their ideas into purpose-driven businesses, brands, and products.

Her journey took a life-altering turn when she was diagnosed with blood cancer. Rather than surrender to fear, Suzanne leaned on her faith in God and her passion for brand building to overcome chemotherapy ~ emerging stronger, more determined, and deeply inspired to help others. She now channels that resilience into empowering women over 40 who are facing unexpected life, health or career challenges, guiding them to reclaim their purpose and launch their dream ventures.

Originally from Cameroon, Suzanne recently relocated to the U.S. to reunite with her daughter.

To discover more about Suzanne's miraculous recovery story, access her E-book on Amazon.

FREE Faith-filled Power Affirmations and Brand Launch Checklist at www.sm-brandin.pro.

FREE Consultation and More Info:
contact suzanne.mouelle@sm-brandin.pro or Scan QR!

The Heart of Healing ~ A Cancer Journey of Transformation

Neelam Ghuliani

The Diagnosis

The air in the sterile doctor's office hung heavy, the silence broken only by the rhythmic tick of the clock on the wall. Dr. Barbara's kind eyes held a sympathy that mirrored the tremor in my own hands. "Stage four, Invasive ductal carcinoma." The words echoed in the cavernous space of my skull, each syllable a death knell to the vibrant life I'd envisioned.

"How much time do I have?" I asked, my voice barely above a whisper.

"Two months if you don't take any treatment," she replied, her clinical tone doing little to soften the blow.

In the days that followed this devastating revelation, the reality of my diagnosis began to manifest in ways I hadn't anticipated. My hair, once a cascade of dark curls that framed my face like a halo, had been my crowning glory. It had been the secret weapon of countless flirtations, the envy of my friends. Now, it was destined to become the first casualty in this cruel war.

A week after the first chemo session, I gingerly ran my fingers through it, feeling the familiar strands detaching in clumps. Panic clawed at my throat. In the sterile white of the shower, I sank to the floor, the lukewarm water washing away not just the clinging remnants of fallen hair, but also the tears that streamed down my face.

"Why me?" I screamed into the empty space with sheer anger, my voice a hoarse echo. What cosmic debt had I incurred to deserve this? The future I'd meticulously built ~ my wedding bells, the promotion at work, my trip to Italy ~ all dissolved like mirages in the desert heat.

This wasn't supposed to happen. Not to me. Not at 40. I wasn't ready to relinquish the reins of my life, to become a passenger on a journey to an unknown destination. But the relentless reality was this ~ the cancer was in charge now, dictating the pace, the treatment, the very rhythm of my breath.

Yet even in this moment of profound despair, something began to stir within me. As I rose from the cold tile floor, a steely resolve replaced despair. Grief would have its time, but not today. Today, I would fight. I would fight for every stolen strand of hair and every stolen dream. This wasn't the ending, it was just a detour ~ a forced march on a different path. I would reclaim my life, one stolen moment at a time. The battle had just begun, and I, a warrior with a bald head and a heart full of fire, was ready.

THE BATTLE WITHIN

What followed was my descent into a war zone I never could have imagined. Two rounds in, battles waged against a foe that burrowed deep within. Each chemo session felt like a meticulous demolition inside me. My body, once a temple of vibrant life, now resembled a battlefield littered with the debris of fatigue and pain.

My once-luscious hair, a testament to my vanity, had surrendered, leaving scant peach fuzz. A wig became the veil to cover my insecurities – a desperate attempt to mask my lack of self-love and acceptance. Meanwhile, food, once a source of joy, became the enemy. Herceptin,[7] my supposed savior, turned traitor, unleashed a relentless wave of nausea that left me clinging to the porcelain throne, my insides churning in a grotesque ballet. Steroids, another supposed ally, brought a different kind of torture – bloating that felt like my body was being inflated from the inside, a constant, dull ache.

Even sleep, my last refuge, offered no escape. I felt like thousands of tiny, sharp needles were continuously pricking across every inch of my body. My once peaceful haven of dreams turned into a battleground of restless nights and bone-deep fatigue.

As weeks turned into months, the cumulative effect of this assault began to take its toll on more than my physical body. Looking in the mirror, I barely recognized the woman staring back. The vibrant spark in my eyes had dimmed, replaced by a hollow despair. The will to fight, once a fiery ember, flickered precariously on the verge of extinction.

But this time, the question felt different. Lying there, eyes fixed on the ceiling, it escaped as a ragged whisper: "Why?"— "Why such suffering?" Silence followed. No booming voice. No divine explanation. Just the steady hum of fear, quiet yet unrelenting, a reminder of the fragile thread I was holding on to.

Yet in that silence, something shifted – subtle but undeniable. The anger and despair that had consumed me began to soften, giving way to quiet acceptance. This wasn't the life I had planned, but it was the life I was living now. Maybe the fight was no longer about winning. Maybe it was about finding a sliver of peace in the chaos, a flicker of hope in the dark.

---

[7] Herceptin treats HER2-positive breast cancer by blocking overactive HER2 receptors, slowing tumor growth and improving survival.

Maybe it was about enduring. One agonizing breath, one searing cramp, one excruciating moment at a time. Maybe it was about clinging to the love that surrounded me ~ unwavering support, the silent prayers of family, and the whispers of hope from friends.

The battle wasn't over. But in the quiet of that morning, a small spark reignited. It wasn't the fiery inferno of defiance it once was, but a flicker, a fragile ember of hope that refused to be extinguished. It was enough. For now, it was enough.

THE ANTS OF PAIN

This newfound acceptance would soon be tested by what became one of my most harrowing experiences. The silence of the house pressed against me, as heavy as the leaden blanket of pain that draped my body. My dark grey sofa ~ once a comfort, now just a witness to my silent suffering ~ held me like a newborn baby, barely containing the storm raging inside my veins.

The fourth chemotherapy coursed through me like an army of microscopic soldiers wearing boots armed with razor-sharp spikes. Relentlessly they marched—up and down my limbs and through my bones, piercing every cell with each merciless step. Thousands of tiny ants trampled my insides in a calculated, devastating rhythm ~ each step a piercing scream, a silent agony that trembled beneath my skin.

My eyes, barely open, were just tiny slits allowing the thinnest slivers of afternoon light to penetrate. In this state of profound vulnerability, I grasped at anything that might anchor me to hope. Outside my patio, the old oak tree stood sentinel ~ its massive trunk a silent guardian, its branches reaching out like protective arms. I focused on its steadiness, its rootedness. While my body felt like it was disintegrating from the inside, that oak remained unshaken, unwavering.

Language failed. How could words describe this excruciating internal massacre? It wasn't just physical ~ it was a profound, cellular devastation. Each breath was a negotiation, each heartbeat a small miracle. The chemo was supposed to save me, yet it felt like a controlled demolition of everything I was or ever would be.

I was alone, but gradually, the world outside my window began to offer solace. The oak became my companion, its leaves rustling with a gentle whisper that seemed to say, "Endure. Just endure." And so I did. The wind chimes hanging on the patio began to softly sing, their delicate melody a whisper of comfort. Their sound was like my mother's voice, gentle and reassuring. Though she had passed, I could feel her presence close by ~ not as a physical touch, but as a spiritual embrace. Each tinkling note was a caress, a reminder that I was not truly alone.

My body trembled as the ants continued their brutal march, their spikes tearing through my internal landscape. But the oak tree remained, the wind chimes continued their soft song, and somewhere deep within me, a spark of resilience flickered ~ refusing to be extinguished.

In this moment of profound vulnerability, I was both broken and unbreakable. My body was a battlefield, and I was both the war and the warrior. Yet this experience, as brutal as it was, was preparing me for what would become the most crucial moment of my entire journey.

THE TURNING POINT

What came next would test everything I thought I knew about surrender and resilience. The fifth round of chemotherapy broke something inside me. Not just my body—which felt like a battlefield of microscopic wars—but my spirit. I was done. Exhausted. The nausea was an endless tide, drowning me in waves of despair that crashed relentlessly against my fragile hope.

The chemotherapy had become so aggressive, so overwhelming, that it had stripped away even my most fundamental practices. My meditation—something I had cultivated for years as my lifeline—was now beyond my reach. I couldn't concentrate, couldn't sit still, couldn't find that sacred space within myself that had always been my refuge. The very practice that had sustained me through life's challenges had been obliterated by the chemical assault on my system.

In that moment of absolute surrender, I closed my eyes and reached out to my spiritual guide, Babuji. "Take me," I whispered. "I cannot fight anymore." The room was heavy with my defeat, the silence punctuated only by my shallow breathing.

Just then, as if summoned by some divine intervention, my friend Hema called. I didn't hide my despair. "I'm finished," I told her, my voice a thin thread. "I want to go to Babuji's divine world."

There was a pause. Then Hema's voice ~ firm and loving, refusing to let me sink. "No, Neelam," she said. "Not like this."

What happened next would become a turning point that shifted everything. She began listing vegetables. Carrots, fennel root, cucumber, beet, turmeric, tomato, celery, ginger, zucchini. A litany of potential healing. But I was beyond lectures, beyond hope. "No use," I muttered. "If you want to help me, show me. Tell me why. Prove to me there's a reason to keep fighting."

I didn't expect what came next.

Within hours, Hema appeared at my doorstep. Her bicycle leaned against the wall; a small bag clutched in her hands. No judgment in her eyes, just pure determination. She didn't speak much. Instead, she began to wash, chop, and transform those richly colored vegetables into liquid hope.

The Omega juicer hummed to life, a mechanical symphony of healing. Vibrant colors swirled, each vegetable bringing its own medicine ~ carrots for immunity, beets to purify blood, celery for inflammation, ginger to quell nausea, turmeric to fight cancer. Not a lecture, but a living demonstration of hope.

By the time she finished, she had not just made *one* juice, but prepared weekly bags, pre-portioned, waiting to be transformed into liquid strength. "For when others visit," she said simply. "So they can help you too."

In that moment, something shifted. Not a dramatic transformation, but a subtle realignment. Hope wasn't about complete healing. It was about this ~ a friend who would bike across town, stand in my kitchen, and fight for my life when I had stopped fighting for myself.

The juice was more than nutrition. It was love, distilled into its purest form. And as I sipped that first glass, I began to understand that healing would require more than just battling the disease ~ it would demand a fundamental shift in how I viewed myself and my worth.

But there was another dimension to my brokenness that Hema's practical love couldn't directly address. My meditation practice—the spiritual foundation I had built over decades—lay in ruins. The chemotherapy had not only ravaged my body but had also severed my connection to the inner sanctuary I had cultivated since 1992. I simply couldn't meditate on my own anymore; the treatments had left me too scattered, too depleted, too overwhelmed.

It was then that my friend Beena, a preceptor from the Heartfulness Institute, stepped in like a guardian angel. Recognizing the depth of my spiritual crisis, she made an extraordinary decision. "I'm going to give you one-on-one meditations," she said simply. "You don't have to do anything but receive."

What followed was a form of grace I had never experienced. Every Friday at 9 AM, Beena would arrive like clockwork, her presence a beacon of consistency in the chaos of my treatment schedule. She would sit with me, her presence holding space for what I could no longer access alone. Through her guided meditations, she became a bridge back to my own heart when I couldn't find the way myself. In these sacred Friday morning sessions, I didn't have to struggle or perform or maintain anything ~ I could simply be held in the field of divine grace.

These individual sessions became a lifeline, slowly nursing me back to my spiritual practice when everything else had failed. Through Beena's generous heart and divine guidance, I began to remember who I was beneath the devastation of treatment. She didn't just offer me meditation ~ she offered me a way back to myself.

THE GLASS CUP

This realization led me to one of the most profound insights of my journey. In the early days of my diagnosis, I felt that I was like a cup riddled with cracks and holes, constantly trying to fill myself with love and validation from others. I begged, I pleaded, I reached out desperately for someone to fill me up. But the more I sought external validation, the emptier I felt, as everything I received leaked through the cracks of my self-doubt.

One sleepless night, during the depths of my treatment, a realization dawned on me. I had been approaching life backward.

I had been seeking to be filled by others when I should have been learning to fill myself first.

The next morning, inspired by this newfound understanding, I took an actual glass cup from my cabinet and placed it on my bedside table. It became my daily visual reminder to fill my own cup first. Every morning, I would look at it and ask myself: "What will fill my cup today? What small act of self-love can I offer myself?"

Some days, it was as simple as five minutes of meditation. Other days, it meant saying "no" to a visitor when my body needed rest. Sometimes it meant allowing myself to cry, to feel the full range of my emotions without judgment. Gradually, through these small daily acts of self-compassion, I learned that self-love wasn't selfish ~ it was necessary.

As my cup began to fill, something miraculous happened. Instead of desperately seeking love from others, I found I had an overflow to share. The love I gave no longer came from a place of lack but from abundance. This transformation didn't happen overnight, but through consistent practice. I began to understand that true healing required addressing not just the physical aspects of cancer, but the emotional and spiritual wounds that had made me vulnerable in the first place.

Now, years after my cancer journey, the glass cup remains on my bedside table. It reminds me daily that I cannot pour from an empty vessel. To truly serve others, to truly give love, I must first fill my own cup to overflowing. This lesson would prove essential as I began to examine the deeper patterns that had shaped my life.

THE CHAINS OF GRUDGES

As my self-awareness deepened, I began to recognize how profoundly my emotional patterns had contributed to my illness. Cancer became a powerful catalyst, jolting me awake from emotional slumber. Before diagnosis, I carried the weight of old hurts and resentments, living shackled by invisible chains of grudges that kept me bound to the past.

It was through Heartfulness practices and guidance from my spiritual teacher, Babuji, that I received what felt like divine insight: this journey was meant to ignite inner awakening. As I deepened into this understanding, I realized that cancer had arrived as a rebirth experience, forcing me awake after years of self-neglect.

Looking back with this new clarity, I could see how I had been desperately empty, seeking love and validation from others to fill the void within. Yet whenever I begged for external validation, I encountered only rejection, which deepened my wounds and strengthened my chains. This pattern had become a prison of my own making.

This recognition led me to a crucial moment of reckoning. "Why do I need others to accept me?" I asked myself one night, staring at my reflection ~ bald, gaunt, but somehow more visible than ever before. The irony wasn't lost on me. Once, I had been vain about my hair, attaching my worth to its thickness and shine. Now, having been forced to let it all go, I found something far more enduring beneath the surface.

Through this process of letting go, I came to understand that new growth emerges from chaos; destruction becomes the necessary condition for new patterns to form. What struck me most profoundly was that self-love wasn't just a pleasant concept but the urgent lesson my soul needed to learn. Each experience, I realized, is exactly what we need to learn from, and the code to decipher it is remarkably simple: love your thoughts, your body, your mind, your experiences, and most of all, your heart.

As this understanding deepened, the chains that once bound me—resentment, self-criticism, dependence on others' approval—began breaking, one by one, through radical self-acceptance. With each broken chain, I could see my life's purpose more clearly, finally understanding that my stories of rejection were actually lessons in resilience waiting to be uncovered.

Yet my journey of rising from illness was never easy. The choices available to me at the lowest point seemed painfully limited, and for me, rising above was my only option. Through this struggle, I discovered that resilience isn't about avoiding others' judgments but rather about developing immunity to their power over me.

This led me to wonder: is resilience innate or learned? I found it's both. Resilience is a latent seed within us that must be consciously cultivated. For the longest time, I had pursued it like a mirage, something tantalizingly close yet always beyond my grasp. Until one transformative day, I realized resilience wasn't something to chase but something to embody, moment by moment, breath by breath. This realization led me to establish practices that would sustain this transformation.

THE DAILY RHYTHM

Understanding that lasting change requires consistent practice, I established what became the heartbeat of my healing journey ~ the daily rhythm of Heartfulness practices that structured my life with purpose and presence. Each morning dawned with meditation. I sat in stillness, not merely cultivating positive thoughts, but deeply connecting with my heart's authentic intentions and values for the hours ahead.

As the day unfolded, I practiced mindful awareness through deliberate heart check-ins ~ brief sacred pauses before decisions or during moments of overwhelm that gently guided me back to my center when treatments and fears pulled me into chaos. These moments of conscious connection became lifelines, anchoring me to what truly mattered beyond the immediate crisis.

When evening shadows lengthened, I engaged in the powerful Heartfulness cleaning practice. I consciously released the day's accumulated tensions and impressions from my system, before concluding with gratitude and surrender ~ a profound offering of both my joys and struggles to something greater than myself. This consistent rhythm created a sanctuary of peace within the storm of cancer, anchoring me to what truly mattered beyond the diagnosis.

What I discovered through this daily practice was that healing wasn't just about fighting disease ~ it was about creating a life structure that supported my highest self.

THE TRANSFORMATION

Today, I move forward with my genuine smile, having scaled formidable barriers that once seemed insurmountable. Cancer arrived not as an enemy but as an unexpected teacher, jolting me awake to examine my soul's deepest chambers.

The woman who once desperately sought others' approval now stands rooted in her inherent worth. The woman who once defined beauty through lustrous hair now recognizes that true radiance emanates from an open heart. The woman who once cried, "Why me?" now embraces the mystery, understanding that wisdom often dwells not in answers but in living the questions.

My hair returned with a new texture and resilience that mirrors my inner rebirth. My body wears its scars like sacred text chronicling battles fought in darkness and light. My heart, once shattered by the need for validation, now beats with expanded capacity for compassion ~ both for myself and for others.

Looking back, I can see that cancer became a catalyst for cultivating resilience and self-love. The oak outside my window remains, its branches cherished companions that witnessed my rebirth. The wind chimes continue their gentle melody, reminding me that presence transcends physical form. My glass cup sits, brimming with love that begins within and radiates outward, a daily reminder of the profound shift from seeking to giving.

This story transcends "conquering" cancer ~ it chronicles transformation through embracing it fully. Daily Heartfulness practices continue to sustain this unfoldment: morning meditations, mindful pauses, and evening gratitude that complete each cycle of growth. I continue evolving not despite my cancer experience, but because of the profound awakening it initiated.

About Neelam Ghuliani

My life's purpose is harmonizing heart and mind. Since 1992, I've practiced Heartfulness, and since 2007, I've volunteered to share it freely ~ just as it was given to me. I guide others toward inner balance while pioneering technological innovations that serve humanity.

My commitment to service manifests through fundraising for children with Asha for Education and Child Relief & You, building homes with Habitat for Humanity, and empowering others through Toastmasters and the Project Management Institute. Each role reflects my dedication to lifting others while walking my own path of growth.

My academic journey—Stanford Innovation & Entrepreneurship Program & AI certification, BSEE/MSEE from San José State, and MBA from UC Santa Cruz—represents my pursuit of knowledge that bridges technological advancement with human-centered values.

Professionally, I develop AI solutions for energy, healthcare, medical devices, and pharmaceutical industries, not merely for efficiency, but to create space for deeper human connection. I build high-performing teams where both technical excellence and compassion thrive.

My purpose is crystal clear: to demonstrate how technology, guided by mindfulness and heart-centered wisdom, can transform our world while honoring our shared humanity.

Get early updates on my next book! ~ Stories and lessons from my cancer journey blended with the Heartfulness practices that helped me heal and transform. **linktr.ee/neelamghuliani**

Spiritual Awakening
and
Inner Grace

Chapter 4

LEARNING TO LIVE THROUGH THE EYES OF MY SOUL

Mara Schachter

When I was a child, I had a highly sensitive nature and an open third eye. I was seven when I received my first visitation from the spirit realm.

In a vision, a friendly, wise old owl came to my bedroom window in the middle of the night. The owl was as real to me as if I was seeing it with my physical eyes. As if beckoned, I climbed onto its back, and together we flew, turning left through the side of my house toward my backyard. I could feel every flap of its wings as we glided through the air. This felt different than a typical dream. It was visceral and exceptionally vivid. This was my first conscious third eye experience.

As we flew through the side of my house, I recognized our location, but at the same moment, the familiar morphed into something extraordinary before my eyes. The boundaries of the mundane world ~ with its garbage bins, hockey sticks and snow shovels ~ dissolved. The night was deep and dark... the land filled with shadows and the sky pitch black.

Before us was a dark forest with tangled vines and trees like gnarled hands. The owl flew swiftly through the wood, deftly weaving in and out of the thorny branches. Despite the other-worldly scene, I felt safe on the owl's back, trusting its guidance.

Crossing the threshold of the backyard revealed an entirely different scene: the dark forest suddenly vanished, replaced with the bright light of the sun. My backyard was lit up, as if in technicolour, with its green grass and blue skies. I could feel the warmth of the sun on my skin. In the center of the yard was a blazing bonfire, its flames rising high into the sky. There were children skipping merrily around the fire, each holding a sparkler in their hand, waving their own small flame as they danced about. Hearing the sounds of their laughter, I felt light, carefree and happy.

At the time, I couldn't integrate the vision, but I knew it was important because the owl visited me three times that same year, showing me exactly the same thing each time. Only now, over thirty years later, can I begin to decode the owl's visit. It opened my channel to spirit, and foreshadowed one of the main themes of my life: transmuting darkness to light, transiting between these dualities and integrating them to wholeness. The owl initiated me into the realm of the soul, the shadow, and the deeper mysteries.

Owl has the power to see in the dark. The owl gave me this gift. After that first vision, my supersensory channels opened, basically overnight. This opening didn't just look like friendly fairies or rainbow coloured angelics. It also came bearing down on me with an emotional weight that shook me to my core.

I became hypersensitive to everything ~ and everyone ~ around me. I always knew when my brother felt happy or frustrated, or when my mother felt calm or angry, even when they didn't express their emotions. I felt their emotions *inside* of me. But I wasn't aware this mechanism was happening, so I interpreted what I felt from other people as my *own* thoughts and emotions, often leaving me overwhelmed and anxious.

I started to see things in the night ~ with my physical eyes ~ when I was alone in the dark and quiet. It terrified me. When I was around nine years old, I saw a poltergeist. I awoke suddenly in the middle of the night. As I peered into the hallway through my open bedroom door, I saw a male figure walking slowly toward my bedroom, his silhouette illuminated in neon green. My whole body jolted in fear. My heart beat so fast. I couldn't breathe. Cold sweat enveloped me from head to toe. Sheer terror reverberated through me as I quickly threw the bed covers over my head.

For years, I slept like that every night ~ paralyzed, hiding under the covers, not daring to make a sound for fear it was coming for me. I was too terrified to even peek out, so afraid of what I would see. I would work up the courage to poke my nose out to take in a quick breath, only to instantly take shelter under the covers again. Many nights, I would crawl into my brother's room and sleep there. It was the only thing that made me feel safe in the dark.

Fear closed my third eye, but I now see how wise my young self was to close it at that tender age. I believe that without the knowledge to understand these types of experiences, or the adult wisdom to process them, it can be far too much for a child's nervous system to hold. I now understand that deep cellular memories were being activated within me from lifetimes of wounding, triggering fear that would take me decades to process, integrate and heal. *This* was the shadow world the wise old owl had prepared me to enter.

We experience a fearful event, a moment that triggers fear; but existing in a perpetual state of *afraidness* is different. My experience with fear was like that. It lived in my body and my mind perpetually reactivated it. Fear was like luggage; I carried it with me for years. But it has also been one of my greatest teachers.

Seeing the apparition was terrifying, but it also cracked me open to the truth that our human experience is so much more than what it appears to be on the surface. This catalyzed a lifelong spiritual hunger for the truth of our reality, the expansion of my consciousness, and a relationship with God. Without this experience, I wouldn't have forged my self-healing journey, opened my spiritual channels, or learned how to use those gifts in service of others.

Fear maintained its grip on me throughout my teens and twenties, creating a deep subconscious desire for safety. To adapt and protect myself, I subconsciously sought safety through a myriad of maladaptive defense strategies.

One such strategy was people pleasing ~ if I pleased others, maybe that would help me feel safe.

My subconscious thoughts would have sounded like: *"If the people around me are happy, then I will feel happy, so I can feel safe. If I avoid conflict and confrontation, I won't feel the negativity of others, so I will feel safe."*

I packaged myself to be digestible to others: *"If I can be who others want me to be, I will be liked, then I will feel safe. If I dim my light, and don't shine too brightly, I won't attract the darkness of others, so I can feel safe."*

So, when my mother told me countless times that I was too sensitive, I shoved my emotions deep down inside and tried to be "good." I internalized this label, believing that it wasn't acceptable to express myself, and that my emotions were too much for people to handle, which ultimately meant *I* was too much to handle. So I dimmed my light, kept myself small, and took up less space. I would take the emotional temperature of a room as I entered it to gauge how I would show up, to match the energy rather than radiate my own. But deep in my core, I yearned to authentically express my real self.

After graduating University in my early twenties, I struggled with my next steps. Having studied what interested me in my Bachelor of Arts degree, majoring in Theatre and Humanistic Studies and minoring in Religion, my plan was to move to New York after graduation and continue to study acting. But my fear was stronger than my passion, and my desire for safety stronger than my will to pursue my dream.

I ended up moving back to Toronto with Robbie, my boyfriend at the time and now my beloved husband. He lovingly supported me mentally, emotionally and financially over the next few years as I struggled to find my direction. I even considered going to law school because that's what I thought I "should" do, because my grandfather was a lawyer. Ultimately, no career choice felt right, because what I had chosen was safety over personal expression. The hidden inner voice that said, *"If I keep small enough to stay within the boxes that are acceptable for me to inhabit, I will feel safe,"* ultimately won out.

That's when the panic attacks started. By then, I was working in an advertising career that was, to put it mildly, not a fit. I stayed small and largely hidden in my job. I felt like a caged bird, doing time, sentenced to an adult life not entirely of my choosing.

As a panic attack struck, it felt like the ground beneath my feet was giving way. The world around me would start to spin, then a sheet of cold sweat enveloped my body all at once. My mouth suddenly turned to cotton, my tongue so sticky I could hardly speak. My heart raced from adrenaline, making me want to get up and pace, only to find my feet like lead weights, defying my attempts to move. Then came what was, for me, the scariest symptom of all ~ not being able to catch my breath, the inflamed sensation in my chest leaving me gasping for air.

"This is it. I'm dying."

I would anxiously plead to Robbie, "Take me to the hospital! Something is really wrong!"

Grounded and calm as ever, he would look me in the eye and reassure me, "You are ok. Just sit with your back against the wall and breathe. This will pass."

Each time, it was the same. I would sit in our ensuite bathroom with my back up against the wall, listen to the sound of his voice, dim the lights, and pray to God for it to pass.

I now understand the panic attacks were a message from my soul. It was revolting against the suffering I had been putting it through. I had suppressed its truth and expression, and dimmed its light for too long! It was time to liberate, unmask, and break free from limitation! Even then, I had a deep inner knowing that I was being guided *by* something, *to* something, *for* something greater than me. But in the words of Carl Jung, "If the path before you is clear, you're probably on someone else's."

At 30, while pregnant with my first son, everything began to shift. When a mother is carrying a child in her womb, two souls reside in one body. A soul in the womb is untouched by the illusions of this world: they are protected, peaceful, in bliss. While in utero, my son's energy felt like that... so high vibration and pure. I was physically so ill during my pregnancy with him, with morning sickness that lasted all day ~ but exchanging energy with him while we shared my body made me feel blissed out. His energy connecting with mine brought new thoughts.

I started to ask myself questions like *"What is my purpose? What brings me joy? How can I connect more deeply with my intuition?"*

He was helping me let go of pleasing others at my own expense, and shrinking myself to fit inside boxes. He ultimately was the catalyst that prompted me to begin releasing the fear that remained locked in my body, making me want to stay hidden ~ just like I did as a child ~ under the covers. I knew, deep down, I was being ushered into reopening my connection with spirit, and that I would have to overcome my fears to do so.

At 32, while pregnant with my second son, my spiritual gifts completely reopened. His soul revealed many things to me, including some of his past lives. I could feel when his soul was in his body, and when it was traveling the galaxy. The energetic exchanges between my soul and the souls of my two beautiful boys opened my heart to pure love in a way I'd never known. In recognizing their divine magnificence, I began to see my own.

As they grew inside me, I grew alongside them. I started to feel like myself again ~ renewed, energized, and more empowered than ever to make the changes in my life that my soul had been urging me to make. I left my career and began taking energy classes. I learned how it felt to be in my own energy, to charge and de-charge energy, and to connect with divine energy and be a bridge for others to experience that too. I felt grounded, embodied, and excited about life again.

My children gave me the courage to reclaim those parts of myself that I had long feared and hidden away. Their births were the portal that took me from the darkness of the shadowed forest to the bright light of my backyard. I believe they were the laughing, dancing children around the fire from the owl's vision. Motherhood continues to reveal the sweetness of life, and an understanding of the Divine Mother's love for all of us, as we are all *her* children.

When I was 36, already a practicing Intuitive helping a small clientele one-on-one, a new guide from the inner planes came into my life. In the early morning hours, in a liminal state between sleep and awake, I had a third eye vision. Similar to the owl vision, this was not a dream, but a vivid, sensory experience.

I found myself standing amongst a heavenly sea of misty white clouds. Approaching me was a beautiful, ethereal, young Indian man with kind eyes. His white robe contrasted with the warmth of his golden skin. We didn't exchange words. Our communication was through the heart. He felt familiar to me; it was not an introduction, but a reunion. He put his right hand over my heart and I felt a surge of electric energy run through me. Then bliss. Pure bliss. It was unlike anything I'd ever felt before. I felt like I had been lit up from the inside. The feeling lasted long after the experience.

Shortly after, through several serendipitous events, I found myself on the website of Marguerite Rigoglioso, PhD. She was sharing ancient teachings on the Holy Womb Chakra, which she learned from the Divine Mother Center, the western ashram of the late Hindu saint Sri Sai Kaleshwara Swami (1973-2012). This information, etched on ancient palm leaf manuscripts, was shared in recent times by Swami.

On Marguerite's website, I saw a small photograph of Swami. Upon seeing his face, that same blissful energy surged through me. It was confirmation that he was the saintly man from the vision who had given me what I now understand to be "shaktipat," a transmission of divine grace.

A couple years later, after much research and integration, I began a meditation practice using the mantras that Swami taught from the palm leaf manuscripts. Meditation brought extraordinary experiences, but at the same time, fear started to resurface. It took a magnifying glass to all the repressed fear my subconscious had shielded me from for all those years. I was right back to my trembling, terror stricken inner child, gasping for oxygen in the middle of the night.

Gradually, I was able to sit with the discomfort, and instead of suppressing the fear, allowed myself to feel it. I became conscious of fear as a *pattern* of energy, allowing me to release my attachment to the narratives that fear was creating. By perceiving fear objectively, I identified with it less and less over time. Fear became just like any other emotion: an energy to be experienced that washes over me, like an ocean wave.

I recognized that most of my issues were a symptom of the larger pattern of fear energy that wove its way through my life. This helped me reclaim my personal power and open my heart more deeply to love. The practice of meditation continues to bring clarity of consciousness, strengthen my will, and keep me grounded so I can remain open hearted in an unpredictable world.

During a holiday program with the Divine Mother Center, I experienced a profound heart-opening connection with Jesus' energy in a group meditation. (And yes, I'm a proud Jewish woman with a deep connection with Jesus, but that's a story for a different chapter!) My intention was for Jesus' light to enter my third eye, touch my heart, and help me understand we are all one.

In a vision, he showed me a painful memory. I saw it from above, looking down at myself from a higher perspective. It was my first year at McGill University. I was sitting alone at 3am in the main stairwell on the top floor of my dorm, the entire building quiet with sleep.

This was a very difficult time for me. I had no close friends there and my parents were barely communicating with me. I felt immense social anxiety, living in a communal environment with hardly any privacy. I barely slept, and had lost an unhealthy amount of weight, not having eaten properly for months.

The memory was crystal clear. There I sat, crouched in the stairwell, looking out the large windows that faced the night. The harsh glare of the indoor fluorescent lights reflected off the windows, making the outside scene difficult to see. Everything and everyone I knew felt so far away. I felt lost, forgotten and alone.

"What is wrong with me? Everyone seems to be thriving here, and I can't even function."

Coming out of the vision, I questioned why Jesus had shown me that particular snapshot in my history. A moment later, I understood.

Jesus gifted me with exactly what I didn't know I needed. It was the apex moment of a painful time in my life that I had buried. I never told a soul the full extent of what I went through that year. I had just put on a brave face, struggled on, and pushed through. Until that moment, I hadn't even processed the loneliness and pain that I felt. I only realized how heartbroken I had been, and still was, when Jesus showed me *myself* through *his* eyes.

His vision revealed that I wasn't alone, even in my loneliest moment. I was loved, even in my most shameful moment. Jesus showed me that he was there, and has always been there, especially in my darkest times.

Jesus helped me unearth those long-buried feelings, and by observing them through his eyes, with pure love, the pain melted away. Warm tears flooded my eyes and poured down my face. In that moment, I felt seen, understood, and loved unconditionally. I was healed.

Through Jesus, I learned that when we bring love to our dark, painful places, we transmute them into light. This is an act of self-love we can all do for ourselves. Culturally, we are programmed to believe that love and fear are separate. But nothing is separate from love. So when we love our shadow, it melts away. Our shadows become light when love enters them.

I can't help but connect this revelation to the owl's vision ~ the archetypal theme of darkness and light, traversing *both* aspects of self and integrating them to wholeness. I did my personal healing to uncover my wounds and with love and compassion, faced my fears, which brought these shadowed fragments of self out of the dark and into the light.

That's when I learned the lesson my shadow had been teaching me all along. It's the same lesson your shadow is teaching you: the light we are seeking is already inside of us. It *is* us. The light that is our soul is the flashlight that illuminates our path forward, guiding us to embrace our darkness ~ our fear, shame, anger ~ and when we do, we liberate our light. We become free!

Swami Sri Kaleshwar taught: "In the pure light there is a darkness, and in the darkness there is a light, and when we can see that light in the dark we can connect with the divine." That is *all* of us and *all* of life. We are brought into the shadow world because God wants us to know how brightly we shine, especially in the darkness. We are all being guided along the winding path of our lives in order to become the light we seek.

Having been guided many times in my life, I now have the honour of guiding others along their journey. As an Intuitive and Healer, I serve as a bridge between you and your soul and divine energy. These divine energies guide us to unlock our own sacred intuitive wisdom, break free from emotional pain, rediscover our inner power and create a life of abundance, liberation, satisfaction and joy.

My approach blends ancient healing technologies with modern insights that facilitate healing on the deepest level ~ the level of the soul. My clients and students receive knowledge, practical tools, and inspiration to live unapologetically, authentically and with purpose ~ empowered to embody their light and share it with the world.

A life of miracles is possible when we live through the eyes of our soul.

ABOUT MARA SCHACHTER

Mara Schachter is an Intuitive, Healer and writer who helps people unlock their own healing, sacred intuitive wisdom and highest soul's path. She suppressed her intuition and authentic voice for decades, resulting in years of suffering from anxiety, panic attacks, and an auto-immune disorder.

Forging her own authentic path to healing through ancient meditation techniques and healing modalities, she now uses her divine channel in service of others through personal readings, healings, and group workshops.

Look out for Mara's upcoming book about healing from challenging karmic relationships. She lives in Toronto with her husband, Robbie, and their two sons, Nate and Coby.

https://www.maraschachter.com/
https://www.instagram.com/mara_schachter/
me@maraschachter.com

Chapter 5

A LITTLE GRACE ON LIFE'S PLAYGROUND

Shauntay L. Williams

It's a hot summer day in 1975.

Grace, a December baby, feels like a big 6-year-old, but in reality is a quiet, spindly, five-and-a-half-year-old who looks four. She is visiting her aunt Lee, who lives on the fourth floor of a walk-up apartment building. Grace inhales deeply before she begins the hike up, not liking the climb, but feeling happy to see her cousins. Grace loves being around family. It's what she loves most.

Always observant, she wanders around watching everyone interact. There's a lot going on at her aunt's place today; it's not usually this busy, but Grace loves when it is. Most of the men, and a couple of the women, are in the living room playing cards. The room is filled with the smell of cigarette smoke and the sounds of loud talking and laughter. Grace observes the lively scene and moves on to the kitchen, where it's all women.

Grace watches, mesmerized, as Aunt Lee puts the iron comb in the fire on the stove, separates a small patch of hair of the woman who is sitting in front of her, and places hair grease on it. Her aunt takes the comb off the fire. "Be still." she warns the woman, her cigarette dangling between her lips as she speaks, and pulls the hot comb through the patch of hair to straighten it. Grace takes it all in, the sizzling sound as her aunt pulls the comb through the hair and the smell of hair burning. She wonders if she'll ever get her hair hot combed.

Just then, Aunt Lee spots Grace in the doorway. "Why are you looking so sad? Go play with the other kids."

"Yes Auntie," Grace whispers as she turns and makes her way to her cousin's bedroom.

Standing in the doorway, Grace watches her older cousin, Reesa, playing Monopoly, in awe as Reesa commands the other kids. Grace looks around the room: big kids are on the floor playing, while others sit on the bed and watch. Reesa notices Grace in the doorway. Grace is startled, as she's not trying to be seen.

"You wanna come play with us?" Reesa pats a spot on the floor beside her. Grace looks around at the room full of big kids and takes a step backwards. It feels too scary to step into the room with all those older kids. Besides, she tells herself, *"I'm not good at board games."*

She whispers, "No thank you," and walks off, wishing she was a brave big kid, like Reesa.

Grace wanders out the apartment door and heads downstairs towards the lobby. She can hear children laughing and playing, so she quickly makes her way to the bottom of the landing. As her foot hits the last step, the mound of kids disperse in so many directions ~ and fast ~ when one of them calls out, "Let's play Hide and Seek!" Grace's eyes twinkle as she runs off, full of excitement, to choose her hiding place.

"Come hide with me," her other cousin whispers, and beckons Grace with a wave. Grace, full of confidence and bravery, feels like a big girl as she turns away from her cousin and runs off to hide by herself. She giddily decides on the best hiding place and makes a beeline for it, hoping no one has beaten her to it. Three steps down, around the banister, and she is under the stairwell.

It's way bigger than she imagined it would be. She feels even smaller standing under the stairs.

Grace marvels at seeing the back side of a staircase, and the zig zag it makes in mid-air. And there's a huge window. "*Kinda odd to have a window here,*" she thinks as she looks out to see the side of another building. There's a ledge along the wall, reaching from under the stairs to the window. Grace notices goose bumps on her arms. Even the temperature is different... It's cool here, not like Aunt Lee's apartment or even the lobby right on the other side. She stands as still as she can, taking it all in while holding her breath and listening for any sign that she might be found.

Quiet.

"Where did everyone go?" She wonders if the game ended. Did they even know she was playing?

Alone in the quiet, Grace slowly moves towards the three steps just as Earl bounds down them out of nowhere. Grace stops mid-step and catches her breath. She instantly relaxes, relieved she's been found and hiding in isolation is over. She's ready to be "It" for the next round of Hide And Seek.

As she heads toward the stairs leading to the lobby, Earl grabs her arm and tells her to be quiet. Immediately she realizes the game is not over and they, she and Earl, are hiding together now.

Earl yanks her to face him, his face scrunched up... mean and angry. He speaks through his teeth, "You better not tell anyone or I'll hurt you."

Grace's arm already hurts from his grip. Her eyes glaze over and eyebrows furrow. Everything inside of her wants to scream, but she doesn't. Her body is gripped by confusion and fear. Earl is older, bigger, and his mom owns the building where they are playing, (and where Grace's Auntie lives).

He smirks as he hoists her up on the ledge and unzips her pants. He puts his hand inside her panties. Tears well up in her eyes but don't fall. It's so quiet. The lobby that was brimming with kids being loud, playing, and having fun... is dead silent. Grace looks out the window, the sunlight streams in. Earl takes her down from the ledge, his pants now undone, and forces her to touch his exposed privates. Her heart pounds in her chest, and everything inside of her yells, *"SCREAM!"* She wonders if this is her fault, if maybe she's protecting her aunt by being quiet. Maybe if she screams, no one will hear her anyway.

Out of nowhere, the sound of someone running towards them interrupts the noise of her thoughts and Earl's actions. Earl turns to see who's coming as Grace slides around him, ready to make her escape, but he holds her back once he sees it's just his little brother. The three of them stand facing each other in a small circle. Earl commands his brother to undo his own pants. Grace sees the confusion on his face as he looks up at his big brother. He's younger than her by a year, so Grace feels sorry for him.

"Do it!" Earl barks.

He undoes his pants as told. Earl commands Grace to touch his brother's privates. Turning, she and Earl's little brother lock eyes. His eyes bulge out, his body stiff. She wants to cry, not for herself, but for Earl's little brother.

Just then, a burst of noise floods the area under the stairs as if breaking through a time-space barrier. Laugher returns to the hallway. Earl and his brother take off running, leaving Grace standing alone under the stairwell.

Dazed, she slowly reaches down to zip her pants. Her white cotton panties stop the zipper from going up. She pulls and tugs, but it doesn't budge. Terror rises inside of her. Careful not to be seen, the already small Grace shrinks even further as she makes her way to her big cousin's room.

Grace once again stands in the doorway of Reesa's room. This time she stares at her cousin, silently begging for help. Her hands cover her crotch to both hide, and protect, what's already been done.

Reesa sees her. "What's the matter?" she asks, as she moves toward Grace.

Grace bursts into tears and cries out, "I can't zip up my pants." Bawling uncontrollably, her body trembles as Reesa gently pulls her panties out of the zipper and zips up her pants.

"See, it's okay." She attempts to reassure her, looking Grace in her eyes. Grace nods her head slowly, doing her best to stop crying. Reesa gives her a big hug before going back to playing her board game.

Grace goes about life as if it never happened.

~~~~~~~

A few years later, Grace is happy to move back to the neighborhood where most of her family lives, even though it means changing schools. Her grandmother, Shelly, takes her to her first day of 3rd grade. She walks up the stately stairs to the white school building, holding her grandma's hand. They enter the office and are directed to take a seat.

A jolly woman approaches them and greets her grandmother before turning to Grace to say hi. She directs Grace to follow her. Grace squeezes her grandmother's hand. Her legs feel like spaghetti. Her grandma gently nudges her in the direction of the woman. They enter a small room where Grace is told to take a seat beside the jolly woman. Still not knowing why she's been brought to this room, she sits with her back straight and her hands in her lap, twiddling her thumbs. She works hard to control her knees from knocking; they're so bony, she's self-conscious they can be heard.

The woman takes out a book and places it in front of Grace. "Read."

Grace's heart races and the words on the page begin to move around. She can hear her own voice shaking as she reads out loud. It feels like her entire body is shaking! She wants to stop and ask for another chance, a do over, but the courage to speak up is not there. She wonders, *"Why am I here?"*

She soon learns she was being tested for her reading level. Ending up in the lowest group, ashamed, embarrassed, angry, sad, and betrayed by her own silence, she thinks, *"I know I can read ~ just not out loud in a new place with a stranger."* Feeling trapped and embarrassed every time she meets with her group in the back of the classroom for reading time, she sinks to the standards set for her, deciding she's just not smart.

On her first day in 3rd grade at PS 21, Grace stands in line with her fellow classmates outside their classroom door. Their teacher, Mrs. Robinson, faces them, and in a singsong way, says, "Good morning, class," to which all the children reply, "Good morning, Mrs. Robinson" in the same singsong way. Grace follows suit and sings along. As she walks into her classroom for the first time, she sees the chalkboard... already filled with information and assignments. Her eyes widen as she takes it all in: the wall of windows, the rows of desks, and classmates scrambling to their seats.

Unbreakable Spirit

"Your desk is in the middle row, fifth seat back," Mrs. Robinson points.

Grace moves cautiously, doing her best not to trip and fall or bump into another student's desk. Before she can put her backpack down and take her seat, she hears Mrs. Robinson's stern voice.

"Earl, take your seat!"

Grace's heart pounds in her chest. She stands, paralyzed, in the middle aisle. She knows she has to take her seat before she is given the same command, but fear has a grip on her. Afraid to turn around to see if it's the same Earl from under the stairs, she forces herself to slowly turn her head to see. Relief washes over her. It isn't THAT Earl. As her body lets go of the panic, she takes a breath and sits down across from her classmate, Earl. Being in class with someone named Earl makes her think of the other Earl. Her young mind wonders if someone had hurt him and that's why he hurt her. She makes a vow to not hurt ~ as much as possible ~ SHE would not hurt.

Recess is loud at her new school. Kids scream and push past her, running to be the first on their favorite playground ride: swing, seesaw, monkey bars. Some kids just run in circles and scream. Grace feels the rush of excitement and wants to be a part of it. She desperately wants to play and run free, but every afternoon she walks like a zombie straight to the bench and sits down.

Like clockwork, her classmate, Regina, approaches the bench and asks her to play. Regina's smile sparkles with kindness. Inside, Grace jumps with excitement to get off the bench and play ~ happy that Regina is asking. Yet, she shakes her head *no* and watches Regina run off to play.

This daily game with Regina pains Grace. Each time, she whispers to herself, *"Please, please, please ask me again tomorrow,"* always hoping tomorrow will be different and she will say "Yes!" to getting off the bench to play. It feels like there is a large hand inside of her, holding her back, reminding her it's not safe to play. Gripped by fear, many tomorrows come and go, each one leaving Grace worried that one day, Regina will stop asking.

One particular day, after Regina makes her invitation, Grace watches her walk away and knows something has to change or she will be trapped on the bench for all of 3rd grade... maybe all of elementary school. Grace looks across the playground. She sees chaos everywhere: kids jumping rope, others running and colliding into each other, balls flying through the air and rolling on the ground. She looks past the madness that is the playground, and focuses on the seesaws, way across the park from her. They are calling her. Everything between her and the seesaws slows down and gets quiet.

She stands in slow motion and begins to walk past the jump ropes that she previously feared would hit her. The balls fly over her head and in front of her face ~ but she is locked in and moving. Each step gives her more courage. She moves through the minefield of school kids. Arriving at the seesaws unscathed, she is immediately invited to join in and play. And she does! From that day on, nothing keeps Grace off of that playground. Recess becomes her freedom ~ her favorite time of day, when she enjoys being a part of the playground chaos and all of the games.

~~~~~~~

In elementary school, I learned that the rings we observe in a tree stump tell us how old a tree is. I always thought that was fascinating. Decades later, while working as a hypnotherapist, my certifying instructor used a tree analogy that resonated with me. He said, "The innermost ring of a tree ~ the sapling ~ is still there at the very center of the tree, just like our inner child is still there inside of us."

I marveled that our selves at every age are *right there inside of us*. As we grow around that precious one and all of their ideas, beliefs, and experiences ~ good, bad, true, made up, taught, or imagined ~ our baby saplings are forever at the very core of us. Grace is my sapling, active inside of me, often playing Hide and Seek, ping-ponging between being a social butterfly and a clam.

I am still growing through and healing from all the ways my experience, the summer before I turned 6, impacted my life. The biggest impacts being: the feeling of being trapped inside my own body, shutting down and not speaking up for myself, and the deep fear of being seen... because, in my cellular memory, it's not safe. To stop myself from playing a bigger game in life, I chose to pretend I didn't want more, or that I didn't have more to offer; I convinced myself I would rather sit on the bench of life and watch other people play. Just like little Grace, I would often find myself running, jumping and playing in life ~ only to get fearful and bench myself, taking myself out of the game so often, it became ME.

Just as the tree develops rings each year, each decade, my pattern of giving up on myself carved internal grooves that impact my life and choices. Like a butterfly peeking out of its chrysalis but never fully emerging, I quit when the going was good. I ran in the opposite direction of my fully lived life, playing the game of Hide and Seek within myself, too afraid to play. Afraid of winning. Afraid of losing. I stopped myself at every turn, creating a life with many bouts of depression and wanting to ultimately give up on life itself.

Until one day in my twenties...

I'm lying in bed, depressed, not wanting to get up ~ not even to feed myself. In an attempt to coax myself, I tap my thigh. "Come on, you can do it." I manage to stand, but my body, like a rag doll, falls back down on the bed, limp and lifeless. I feel the only energy left inside of me rising up and out of my body. Panicked, I scream out "NO!" Over and over again, "NO." Tears flow salty like a gazillion drops from the ocean. That's when I hear the words, "*If you don't make yourself happy, I am outta here.*"

I realize in this moment that there is "something" inside of me that doesn't want to just live, but wants to enjoy life. I *know* my Soul isn't willing to stay put inside the myriad boxes I've stuffed myself in for the exchange of "safety." So... I promise myself I will do whatever it takes to be happy.

Often flailing in my promise to my Soul, I recommit to it, sometimes multiple times a day. One day after church, a smiling, bubbly woman approaches me. "Spirit led me to give you this book." I look down at the title: *The Game of Life and How to Play It,* and little Grace in me goes *"Eeeee!"* My sapling tantrums, *"I don't play games. I don't want to play games. A game of life? What kind of book is this?"* All the fears of what it has meant for my little one to play games resurface. I shoot the woman a smile and politely say, "Thank you." The resistance in me is clear: I will *not* be reading this book. Yet, compelled to open up the book, I realize all the ways I'd stopped myself ~ not only from playing games like Monopoly or sports, but that I'd held myself back from playing the most amazing game of all: The Game of Life.

It turns out, all I ever wanted to do was play. Whenever I give myself permission to play ~ without excuses, judgement, or comparison, but to really have fun and play full out ~ play takes me to places that my mind could not have conjured up. When I play, life feels magical. So, like a kid, I blow bubbles, I color in my coloring book, and I dance. I remember the things I loved as a child... and I do those things.

Years later, I would solidify my commitment to myself ~ to enjoy my life every day. No matter what, I would find the joy in my life. As a result of this shift in focus, I began to have more and more joy in my life. It was during this time that I realized I'd been playing for a living! In order to teach medical students communication skills, bedside manner, as well as how to give differential diagnoses and difficult news, I'd play roles as a Standardized Patient. I've done the same type of work at law schools and law firms, doing mock trials, depositions, and interviews. I've used play to teach dental students how to deal with difficult patients, financial advisors how to gather information and make a good impression, and I've worked with professionals learning how to interview children who may have been sexually abused. I realized I'd been using the very thing I felt blocked in to help others do the thing I felt blocked doing ~ I was using play to help people communicate.

Using play to teach and to learn has many positive implications. And it's fun! In the book *PLAY* by Stuart Brown, MD, he says "The opposite of play is not work. It's depression."

I no longer deny my little one her voice, this is the key to my healing and thriving ~ and infusing PLAY into everything I do is my vehicle!

Seriously, laugh ~ just because.

Is there a little one inside of you, frightened, stuck sitting on the sidelines, secretly wanting to play all the games? Whisper to that little one, "Get up. I got your back. You can play again and so much more, because I love you and I will take care of your precious heart."

ABOUT SHAUNTAY L. WILLIAMS

Shauntay enjoys living a patchwork quilt life. She has performed professionally as an actress on stage, film (Commercials, Industrials, and Independent Movies). She has also worked as a standardized patient/client/Improv actor for over 25 years, performing many roles for different organizations including medical schools and law firms, utilizing her acting skills as a teaching tool for communication and other profession-specific skill-building.

Shauntay has a BA in Sociology-based Human Relations from Connecticut College. She completed her 200-hour yoga teacher training with The International Sivananda Yoga Vedanta Centre. In 2010, she became an Interfaith Minister with All Faiths Seminary International.

Shauntay's mission is to empower people to PLAY, and to connect to intuition and inner knowing through practices of playing. She has used the tools of acting, movement, self-hypnosis, journaling, and yoga to break out of her cocoon and let her Spirit soar. She believes life is meant to be enjoyed!

"Life is either a daring adventure or nothing at all."
- Helen Keller

What are you daring today?

Email: Shauntay@theintuitiveplaycoach.com

Website: theintuitiveplaycoach.com

For a free mini course go to: https://linktr.ee/shauntayw111

Mothering Through the Fire

Chapter 6

PAIN WAS THE MIDWIFE, SPIRIT WAS THE MEDICINE:
MY DAUGHTER, SUICIDE, ADDICTION, AND THE BIRTH OF MY POWER

Jaque Hanson LMT, ERYT 500

These are the most uncertain, painful days of my life. The glistening spark of my initiation into the dark night of the soul is being birthed....

The cold night chills my bones. Another night filled with fear and insecurity of what the future will bring. Making dinner. Cleaning up. Andrew, my eleven-year-old, sits engrossed in homework.

The sense of warm, spicy Brazil fades as I hang up from talking to my mother and proceed to process her narcissistic, needy ways.

As if by magic, not even a second after hanging up, the phone rings. A firm female voice knocks the wind out of me, "Mrs. Hanson, this is a call regarding your daughter, Jessica. She ran away from the girl's house at the Caron Foundation a little while ago. Please stay by the phone. Our supervisor, Scotty, will be calling you shortly."

I am numb. It feels as if a tomahawk is incessantly chopping into my gut. I stop breathing for a moment. Then, my inner mother-bear comes out of nowhere. I've never felt such a communion of despair interwoven with fear for the survival of my cub, and such frantic need for resolution.

My initiation is crowning, emerging from despair and anguish to reveal my destiny.

YOUTH OF AN OLD SOUL

Growing up near Rio de Janeiro, Brazil, I was driven to reject distractions and focus on meticulously curating a map to a successful, authentic life. An independent only child, I was proudly nerdy and deeply passionate about life. I had a different group of friends for each of the activities I loved. Classical music, ballet, American pop music, old architecture, theater, and museums ~ I loved them all... and much more. I had no time to waste on nonsense. I was a weird teenager and I owned it, but to my parents, I was an enigma. They had *no idea* how to deal with me.

At six, I knew I saw the world differently. My mother called me an "old lady," but I knew ~ I was an old soul. This was both a gift and a burden, especially when I witnessed her shadow. Despite my sharp mind and quick words, my mother remained unreachable—self-absorbed, draining, ruling over my father. One night at bedtime, she cornered me and tried to gaslight me about what an amazing mother she was. I told her, "If a person is truly amazing, they don't have to say it ~ they just are." I was seven.

Trapped in a child's body, my only escape was education; my only hope ~ freedom. I first visited the U.S. that same year and fell in love with the culture. By 18, I had moved to Pennsylvania to study ~ and spent a life-changing year with my aunt and uncle.

To my complete surprise, I fell in love and got married to my cousin's friend. I was a world apart ~ in rural Amish country, where time slowed but my days marched on. As my spouse pursued an eight-year graduate school dream at Johns Hopkins University while working full time, I provided unwavering support, embracing his vision that became my own.

I drove. I built. I learned. I transformed a fixer-upper into a home, all while stitching together a life in an unfamiliar world. My days were long, but I was happy. It was my passion. I experienced pure joy with first my daughter, and later my son. I was brimming with gratitude. Mothering and creating a comfortable, beautiful, and intellectually stimulating nest made me feel alive.

THE CRUCIBLE OF AWAKENING

The helter-skelter began one afternoon in 2002... when my 15-year-old daughter, Jessica, confessed her drug problem and begged for help. My perfect white-picket-fence life cracked. Blood burned through my veins, my head a smoldering volcano. I was speechless—lost—numb.

"How am I supposed to fix this?"

That summer, my gut had screamed that something was wrong with my daughter, but I couldn't pinpoint it. Her hand was swollen, with a deep cut—never stitched. Years later, she admitted the truth: she'd punched the dealer's door as he tried to keep her from his drugs. Worse, I learned she was cutting, burning herself, and battling bulimia.

I was shocked, thinking, "*I have never used drugs or gotten drunk—ever! How could my daughter be in such a predicament?!*" But I refused to let my anger and fear shatter her.

Later, I learned the reason Jessica told me ~ her boyfriend had given her an ultimatum:

"Either you tell your mom you've been using drugs, spending time with my heroin-addicted, drug-dealing brother behind my back, exposing yourself to dangerous people and situations, and that you nearly killed yourself accidentally, or I will." Jessica was snorting meth and her Adderall medication.

All along, I was clear, concise, and focused on a perfect, effective life. I was delusional about how life ought to be. That life was pierced like an overinflated balloon. Puff...

This was the precious beginning of getting to truly meet my true Self ~ *all* of me. My shadows began crawling out of my subconscious toward the light of day. They tormented me with unimaginable fears and self-judgment. The good family girl who was resolute on a phenomenal life was deflated and obliterated.

"I invested all of myself in my family life, and somehow I failed!"

Broken. Vulnerable. I was in the mystery.

We were fortunate to get Jessica into Caron Treatment Centers[8], a leading drug rehab facility nicknamed *The Magic Mountain*. Although grateful for the support, I was still shattered ~ she had never been away from us. The Sunday services, bimonthly group therapy, plus a heartbreaking three-day crash course on addiction were overwhelming, yet crucial. For days after, I wept for Jessica, and for all the other young patients trapped in similar predicaments, and the unbearable pain their families were enduring. With this education came clarity and a deeper realization of the complexity deepening our family's struggle.

For months, I experienced monumental shame, despair, depression, and anxiety. My yoga practice became one lifeline. Another was my lifelong therapeutic relationship with my piano. Life felt unbearable. My stability began slipping and self-hatred was consuming me. Depression weighed me down, making even getting out of bed excruciating. The emotional pain was so intense, it felt physical. But my son Andrew kept me going; I had to feed him, get him to school, care for him.

---

[8] A well-established provider of addiction and mental health treatment headquartered in Wernersville, PA.

I had been teaching my kids authenticity and vulnerability from a distorted place of logic. I had never learned to accomplish that from my sovereign heart.

When I was 15, stress from my mother had triggered my IBS. During Jessica's four months at Caron, it flared up daily ~ but I had to push through. I researched her diagnoses, learned about addiction, and showed up, no matter what. Somehow, a higher power lifted my spirit, guiding me through each initiatory door with a strength I didn't know I had.

I quickly understood the magnitude of what was happening. Even defeated, disillusioned, cynical about humanity, discouraged, exhausted, and disenchanted, I knew that deep inside, I was held by something greater. Something was awakening within me. I began to see ~ to *know* ~ that the spiritual gifts I'd refused when I was twelve were being offered to me again.

THE SACRED OFFER

Dona Erasmina was a close family friend and a wise High Priestess with her own temple of an Afro-Brazilian religion called Macumba. We often needed her gifts for diverse afflictions.

At twelve, a puzzling illness gripped me. Doctors failed. Through an oracle reading, Dona Erasmina revealed that my mysterious illness was a call to recognize that I was a priestess in the making, awaiting initiation.

I remember that moment clearly. To my surprise, I felt powerfully clear about my needs, and I spoke confidently from a space of authority. "I am too young for this responsibility. I want to be a child now."

She kindly offered me a way out ~ but I knew, with striking clarity, what those duties meant. Since I was 6, I've carried the quiet knowing that I've lived many lives. In that moment, the weight of lifetimes devoted to a sacred path became undeniable.

I felt, over my frail and tiny shoulders, the burdensome responsibility I had taken for many lifetimes. That was one of my defining moments this time around in choosing how to live. However, I enjoyed attending the programs at Dona Erasmina's temple. The work there provided undeniable results. Dona Erasmina's invitation to my initiation opened a powerful portal ~ one that revealed, loud and clear, an unspoken truth about my soul and its boundless capacity. And yet, it was healing for me to say no to it at that time.

I said yes to a ceremony to end my "spiritual responsibilities." I thought then that I was done with that nonsense. I'm grateful that I was mistaken in thinking that it was a once-in-a-lifetime initiation invitation. Thank Goddess I was wrong! At twelve, I rejected spirituality; now, as a desperate mother, I was eager to embody those gifts for Jessica.

THE INITIATION

Back to that wild night in the freezing month of February. The clock was ticking and the temperatures were plummeting. A few minutes later, Scotty called. "Mrs. Hanson, please stay by the phone and keep the line open. Jessica will call you, begging to come home through a collect call from the gas station two miles away."

I stood there, phone in hand, frozen for a moment. Then, suddenly, it felt as if a projector turned on in my third eye.[9] I *saw* Jessica—alone in the woods, crouched at the base of a tree as

---

[9] Ajna, the Third Eye Chakra, is the center of intuition and inner wisdom, located between the eyebrows. Meaning "command" or "perceive" in Sanskrit, it guides us with subtle insight from the higher self. It symbolizes the union of dualities—mind and spirit, human and divine.

the frigid forest closed in menacingly around her. There was a dilapidated shed nearby.

A sacred stream of consciousness inhibited my judgmental and logical mind altogether. I could not feel my body standing. There wasn't a second to be incredulous or doubtful. I was completely immersed in this video playing out in real-time. I had no concerns of feeling crazy or desperate. I simply said, "No, Scotty. She's in the woods near a shed. She is not going to call." Not only did I see it, but there was a lucid download of knowing infused and encoded with the vision. My Jessica was alone in the mountains, in the dark, in near-freezing temperatures, and underdressed.

Scotty never second-guessed me. "I am sending an attending counselor there immediately!" He knew the place I was describing. It happened in seconds, but felt like a distorted time warp. I had no time to process or question myself. I just had to get to the Magic Mountain to find my daughter. Years later I read a book about remote-viewing phenomena.[10] That was what I experienced.

I called my children's father, urgently asking him to return home to stay with our son. I layered myself in winter clothes—I was going to find my daughter. Nothing was going to stop me.

My sense at that moment was that I had seen her in a blood-curdling, treacherous, frozen forest. I could feel the energy of death and danger with every breath. I jumped in the car and took the Turnpike. No traffic until the Reading exit. There was a stillness in the air.

---

[10] Remote-viewing research began at the Stanford Research Institute in Menlo Park, California in 1972.

That night was my initiation. I was once again being invited to embody my inner mystic, healer, and wise guide as I stepped swiftly into my sovereign self.

I didn't have spiritual teachers, enlightened guides, or wise elders. I was often the young one with an old, wise soul ~ the one people turned to for guidance and counsel, trusted to offer clarity. YouTube and other social media did not exist at that time. I didn't own spiritual books or DVDs. I had no one in the physical world to anchor me, hold me, or wipe my tears with the sacred embrace of a sister priestess. Though it was just me in that solitude, I knew there was a divine presence guiding me every step of the way.

Effortlessly, I became a believer. There was no path but to surrender to the energy of passion, show up, see with clarity, question the authorities of medicine and psychology, stir the waters, and make bold decisions from the only place I could count on ~ my heart. I didn't know it then, but it was the only truth I needed. I was simply following my inner compass. One instance after another, I was correct ~ to my surprise! It was uncanny, scary, and weird, and yet all was unfolding in perfection. I was truly, but unknowingly, operating in the mystery. I just desperately wanted to keep my beloved daughter alive and safe.

Scotty called and asked me to stop the car so that he could safely talk to me. The ginormous Reading exit sign by the rest stop towered over me. I anxiously pulled over and felt my heart trying to jump out of my chest. The darkness was complete except for my headlights. Scotty said that the counselor found Jessica exactly where I'd seen her with my third eye. So many emotions flooded my nervous system. My gut constricted. My shoulders were so tight, I could barely breathe. Then, I experienced an overflow of relief followed by tremendous rage. Why did this have to happen to my daughter? Why did this have to destroy our lives further than it already had? After getting used to the dysfunction, and learning to pivot and adapt to this maddening situation, there was now *another* leap into the unknown.

Over the phone, Scotty was very firm with me. "Mrs. Hanson, you may only be here on visiting days and hours." I began to cry and to plead with him to let me see her. As I was talking, I could feel my voice change as tremendous resentment arose. Wow... waves of excruciating emotions peaked and plunged, fusing one into the other. I *needed* to see and feel Jessica in my arms.

Scotty pleaded with me to go home. He had to assess the need for medical intervention. I was both infuriated and grateful for his effectiveness and thoughtfulness.

This is where things got interesting... I was feeling such intense energy moving through me that my whole body felt numb. It was freezing outside, but I felt like I was burning up from the inside. Unlike heat, it felt like I was engulfed in swirling and buzzing energy. I opened the car door. I looked around. The natural world surrounding me seemed, somehow, to be a part of it. I walked to the front of my car, spread my legs wide and anchored my hands on the center of the hood. I began to feel even *more* energy, this time coming up from my feet, up my legs, and overtaking every part of me. I began to bawl and scream bloody murder. Primally and fiercely, my whole being was screaming. Meanwhile, a full-body energetic Roto-Rooter was scouring every part of me ~ from the bottom up, from the inside out. I was incredulous! While this was happening, I existed outside of time and space.

Many months later, I discovered that this was the first, and most dramatic, of many kundalini[11] rising phenomena experiences I would embody.

---

[11] Kundalini energy is often described as a powerful, coiled energy located at the base of the spine. The rising of Kundalini, a profound and life-altering experience, is characterized by heightened awareness, spiritual insights, and a sense of unity with the divine.

After being blasted by the sudden uncoiling of my kundalini, I slowly came back to my body. Monumental sadness emerged. I questioned what to do next. Should I go home, or not? I called Jessica's father to let him know what was unfolding, and that we could sleep that night knowing that she was warm and safe, and that, hopefully, she had all her fingers and toes.

I wasn't sure how many hours she had spent alone on the frigid mountain. Since I had to get out of the Turnpike exit anyway to return home, I chose to go to the nearby Caron campus. I parked in the nearly empty parking lot, facing the little house that was the girls' residence. I saw the light on in her bedroom and felt a tidal wave of gratitude.

My family's hope was alive but bruised. I felt grief, longing for what life used to be like, and anxiety for all that I knew would proceed in the next few weeks, months, and years. But, most importantly, I was shocked by how I was initiated. I knew that there was a purpose. I was terrified of who I was becoming, and at the same time hopeful for this new warrior that I had birthed from my depths. Those gifts, that all my life were burdens, had now shifted into becoming the new me. It felt as if Jessica's survival, and consequently mine, were in the hands of this awakening. My inner knowing, or intuition, became vital. The game was on! Life as I knew it was gone, dead, shattered. My intuition became empirical and took the place of the theoretical.

I attended every single group therapy at Caron. Jessica became so appreciative of us, because she saw, close-up, how horrific the lives of most of the other patients were. She began to treasure our home, her educational opportunities, and all that we had been providing her with.

The Sunday mass at Caron was the most outrageous, caring church service EVER! I attended every Sunday for four months. One large living room of two was converted, in Dr. Caron's original mansion, into a chapel with pews, a centered altar with a microphone, and a video camera. The other large room had an enormous screen televising the mass/AA/AL-ANON meetings.

Father Bill was the most rebellious, present, authentic, and wild catholic priest. I've never witnessed such passion to support, be real, and hold space for each human being who walked through the door. He listened to each person and felt their sorrow and tears intensely. I witnessed inner alchemy taking place in each parent, child, sibling, partner, and friend, which completely shifted my awareness. I was unfolding and evolving through my pain *and* their pain. Vulnerability and humility were earned. The highest octave of compassion and passion kept relentlessly uncoiling from within me. The beginning of my understanding of unconditional love was the sacred nectar.

Through this sacred dance with destiny, I found myself.

Arduous years followed with Jessica. She later shared that I intuitively interrupted many of her suicide attempts by seeking her out spontaneously before and after Caron. My beloved Jessica carries the weight of severe multiple sclerosis, and is a survivor of both rape and suicide attempts. Her journey is marked by relentless challenges, each battle leaving deep scars. The shadows of PTSD linger, but so does her unwavering strength. She has been my technology guru and my music and video creation teacher. Jessica is my biggest cheerleader. She believed in me when I failed to do so ~ countless times.

THE GRACEFUL AND HUMBLE RISE OF THE PHOENIX

After Caron, I rose like a phoenix from the wreckage. My morning practices became sacred lifelines, anchoring me when nothing else could. They still enliven and inspire me today. I am fiercely embracing all of who I am in the remembering of my true self.

Jessica and I attended numerous spiritual trainings. Traveling with her to Malta was beyond amazing! Powerful ancestral, personal, and past life healing, as well as opening to our own Inner-Priestess-Selves crowned our journey. We embodied deep remembering and each unleashed our true soul calling.

I downloaded codes in the ancient temples of Malta[12] that initiated me and ignited the creation of Bee Present Wellness and eventually the Beehive Mystery School. I manifested spiritual trainings across the U.S. and beyond, driven via love. To my amazement and disbelief, years later, two clients begged me to create what I knew in my soul to be a mystery school ~ though they had no idea of the depth of what they were asking of me. Jessica attended the first and second years, becoming one of the initiates. A deeper understanding and sisterhood arose from those two years, and from the mirroring of our strengths.

I also honor my son for his angel-like qualities as an empath. His innocence, divine wisdom, and intuitive presence were, and still are, priceless. After Caron, Andrew always knew when Jessica was experiencing panic attacks. He saw first-hand the devastation and unrest of drug use and suicide attempts. He is very focused on living a healthy and productive life.

Where I stand now, I bless every curve of this perilous road to awakening. No triggers, force, or resistance could hold me back from knowing the soul that dwells within. Every sacred entanglement has been a guiding thread weaving me home to myself. I am the echo of my becoming, forged in the sacred crucible of transcendence.

Every single torturous and treacherous experience I have traversed and had the grace to alchemize is now serving to help

---

[12] The ancient temples in Malta are among the oldest free-standing structures in the world, dating back to approximately 3600-2500 BCE.

others in their humble awakening in my Beehive Mystery School, and in other spiritual offerings online and offline. I am eternally grateful for the unfolding mysteries that fuel my love for being *here*. And I hold this truth for all who walk with me in the alluring path of compassionate ascension.

And so it is!

ABOUT JAQUE HANSON, LMT, ERYT 500

Jaque Hanson is a *fierce* and *compassionate* guide through the soul's deepest metamorphosis. Her path ignited in 2002, when her daughter's suicide attempt cracked open a portal of profound awakening. This heart-shattering moment became a sacred turning point—activating Jaque's intuitive gifts and catapulting her into a life of healing, purpose, and spiritual devotion.

She has since become a vessel of wisdom, weaving together shamanism, energy medicine, esoteric arts, Kundalini Yoga, and Maya Abdominal Therapy into powerful, multidimensional offerings. As the founder and spiritual director of the Beehive Mystery School and Bee Present Wellness, she supports empaths, intuitives, and cycle-breakers to release ancestral burdens, embody their sacred gifts, and rise into their full potential.

Jaque's radiant presence and radical compassion create a field of transformation where deep healing becomes not only possible—but inevitable. She doesn't just teach ~ she awakens. She doesn't just guide ~ she fiercely walks beside you. With every step, she is a catalyst for awakening, inviting you home to yourself: empowered, liberated, and profoundly alive.

It is Jaque's deepest joy to offer this Soul-Filled gift ~ a sacred glimpse into her life's work.

More than a gesture, it's a living transmission of compassion, resilience, courage, and love.

Claim your gift here:

Chapter 7

TOWERING CHIAROSCURO

Lorraine Manzo

It was my fifth day at work as a brand-new high school art teacher and I was preoccupied with concerns over my lesson plans. After my divorce, I returned to college to become an art teacher so I could make a better life for myself and my daughter. At forty years old, I was worried about making a good impression and doing the best job possible.

The high school bell schedule began early, with the first class starting at 7:05 a.m. During my third period prep time, I was on my way to see my director to ask about art supplies.

As I walked past the school library, I was surprised to come across a large group of students and teachers intensely watching a TV perched on a rolling cart. Had this been teacher guided, students would have been seated and organized with notebooks. On her way to the library to investigate, one of my colleagues caught up with me.

"What's going on?" I asked.

"A plane crashed into the World Trade Center," she said. Her gaze widened as she made a slow nod of her head.

Oh no! I thought, remembering the previous attack in 1993 when a group of terrorists had parked a truck filled with explosives in the parking garage of the World Trade Center. Six people had lost their lives and more than a thousand were injured on that terrifying day. Luckily, a dear friend of mine who worked at the Twin Towers had been safe.

I hoped and prayed that this crash was an awful accident. As we approached, I realized why everyone was glued to the TV screen. With a knot in my stomach, my body reacted more quickly than my mind to the shocking images on TV. I found it difficult to process what I was watching. Enormous clouds of black smoke poured out of the North Tower. We watched in horror as another plane flew directly into the South Tower with a colossal explosion.

We realized that this was no accident. Chills went up and down my arms and my stomach felt queasy. Panic escalated as the news reporter informed viewers of the flight numbers involved in the crashes. Flight number 11 hit the North Tower at 8:46 a.m. and Flight 175 hit the South Tower at 9:03 a.m.

One of my colleagues became frantic. "I have to go! My husband is on that plane!" She raced out of the library.

Since we were on Long Island within commuting distance of New York City, many students and staff members had family and friends working at or near the World Trade Center. My initial shock and anxiety worsened once I remembered that my ex-husband and his brother were working on a construction job at Number 5 World Trade Center. I had no idea if they were on the site or not. I could only imagine how overwhelmed and anxious my daughter Marissa, a high school freshman, must have felt about not knowing the whereabouts of her father and uncle.

Within minutes, the high school went into lockdown. At that moment I had to be my public schoolteacher self and I could not get to my daughter. Upon being hired, teachers are required to take an oath known as "In Loco Parentis," Latin for "In place of a parent." I was torn between being there for my daughter, and the hundreds of students that I was responsible for. I was anchored in a sea of teary-eyed students who filled the hallways searching for friends and siblings to connect with.

In 2001, less than half the population owned cell phones. Those who had access to one helped others to make contact with their friends and family. As we headed into lockdown, students had seen the frightening attack in the classroom or in the library. Unfortunately there was no cell phone service or landline service to New York City for many days.

A compassionate veteran teacher approached me. "I've been teaching for thirty years and I've never experienced anything like this," she said." I can't even imagine how you're dealing with this as a new teacher."

The loud thud of the heavy metal push bar on the side door caught my attention. The security guard slowly opened the door halfway to speak with a parent. A group of parents who were denied access at the main office had gathered at the side door of the school building, hoping to pick up their children. As the door opened, sunlight brightened the fluorescent lit hallway. The sweet smell of freshly cut grass wafted in, and I was struck by the duality of being in the midst of a horrific crisis on a picture-perfect sunny day.

A distraught mother pleaded with the security guard. "You don't understand," she said. "My husband works at the World Trade Center. I have to pick up my son. He must be overwhelmed with fear. Let me in now!"

Her story resonated with me as I was worried about my own daughter and my family at the Number 5 World Trade Center site. "Ma'am, I understand how upset you are." The security guard calmly explained. "The school is now in lockdown. We are waiting for instructions as to how to proceed. At the moment, for the sake of security, we will need to account for every student in the building before anyone is released. Please have patience as we deal with this crisis. I'm so sorry, I need to close the door now." He waved the parents off as he carefully closed the door with a long slow scrape of the rubber door sweep.

We were once again trapped in darkness. With tears streaming down her face, Sabrina sobbed. "Ms. A, I have to get home. My dad works at the World Trade Center and my mom must be going crazy. I have to find my older brother. He has his car to take us home."

I tried my best to calm her down. "I know how much you want to be with your family right now. I'm so sorry you're going through this. Please be patient. We are all waiting for instructions. Right now, we have to take attendance in every class so we know exactly who is in the building before anyone can leave."

Once inside the classroom, the door had to be locked. No one was allowed to enter or leave. I took attendance and waited for an administrator to open the door with a key so I could give them my handwritten attendance sheet. The principal announced that she would keep us informed as events unfolded. We were advised to refrain from watching live news coverage with students.

I was just getting to know my students, yet I could see they were all struggling to deal with the fear and anxiety on this somber day. Jake, a 6'3" 9th grader, was leaning by the wall intensely gazing out the window in anticipation of what might be next.

I noticed a quiet student who sat staring blankly, arms crossed and shock in her eyes.

"Amanda, how are you doing?"

She shrugged her shoulders and shook her head. I touched her shoulder gently to show my support. I thought about how concerned I was earlier in the day about my lesson plans. Here we were at 10:00 a.m., in lockdown, dealing with a crisis none of us could have been prepared for.

I grappled with the destruction of my beautiful city. I remembered traveling to visit my grandparents when I was a child, and the magnificent skyline that came into full view as we drove over the Queensboro Bridge. As a young girl I imagined myself as Dorothy from *The Wizard of Oz*, gazing upon the sparkling skyscrapers of Emerald City for the first time. The Twin Towers stood as tall as giants, above all the other skyscrapers. The rectangular buildings wore their geometric facade proudly as Haute Couture. For me, New York has always been the city where dreams can come true. It was where I had lived out my dream of attending art school and becoming an illustrator.

I was at once fully engaged with my students and yet I remembered a similar frightening day from my own childhood that had been filled with overwhelming collective grief. My five-year-old self had been busy working on an art project when an announcement alerted us that the elementary school was closing early. I had looked to my teacher for directions, when I noticed that she had tears in her eyes. In fact, all the adults in the school building were teary eyed or quietly sobbing.

It was November 22, 1963. The tragic day that President John F. Kennedy was assassinated. I remembered my teacher explained to us that something terrible had happened to the President of the United States, but I just didn't really understand what that meant. As I traveled home on the bus, I could see people in their cars or on the street, sobbing and comforting one another. When I arrived home, I was glad to be reunited with my parents and brother. We traveled to be with my grandmother, aunts, uncles and cousins. While I was too young to fully comprehend the gravity of the assassination, I understood that everyone

I encountered was heartbroken over the loss of the beloved President of the United States.

Now, on September 11, 2001, I was the teacher responsible for helping my students manage a traumatic event. I told my students that doodling or drawing in their sketchbooks could be therapeutic as we waited for instructions as to how to proceed. Today would be a free drawing day. I encouraged my students to draw any imagery that was best for them. Nick got busy working on a composition of the Twin Towers. His drawings were the majestic Twin Towers as they appeared prior to the explosion. Most of the students created positive images such as peace signs and American flags. As students focused on their art, the energy in the classroom shifted. Chiaroscuro, an Italian art term describing high contrast between dark and light affecting a composition, was apparent in the students' artwork as well as their emotional landscape.

When my classroom phone rang, I was glad to receive a message from my mother. Once Marissa was released from school for early dismissal, she planned to go straight to her grandmother's house. Knowing that my daughter would be taken care of, I sighed with relief.

Addison approached me with the question that was on everyone's mind. "What's going to happen to us?"

"Addison, I really can't answer that question. What I can tell you is that here in school, your safety is the utmost priority. We will do everything we can to make sure you are safe."

Addison took a moment to consider my answer before returning to his seat. I saw him reporting back to his group of friends, who nodded in acceptance of my response.

I appeared calm on the outside to my students, but on the inside I was heartbroken for those who lost their lives and those who were trapped in the Twin Towers.

I had enjoyed the exhilarating views from the outdoor observation rooftop of the Towers on a clear day. I felt as if I was on top of the world, awed by an unobstructed view for 45 miles in all directions. The exaggerated perspective looking down from the top of the Towers was unlike anything I had ever seen.

Inside the Towers, I stepped down to a platform similar to a window seat. Instead of sitting, visitors were invited to hold on to a guard rail and stand right next to the window. Looking down from that extreme height without any barrier felt like I was in free fall. In that moment, I could feel "The Call of the Void," the desire to merge with vast, open space.

When I taught students about one point perspective, I showed them how to draw a dot as a vanishing point and how to add two vertical lines in a "V" shape. Looking down from the top of the Towers was just like that "V" shape. The design of the vertical lines and windows on the buildings made the perspective even more dramatic.

Knowing the physicality of the Twin Towers, I had great empathy for the victims of the attack. I thought about how the workers at the World Trade Center were just beginning their day, maybe sharing a cup of coffee with a colleague or preparing for a morning meeting. Instead, they were victims of a brutal attack and trying to find a way to survive. I quietly grieved and prayed for them.

I was startled when I heard the loud bell signaling an announcement from the principal. We were informed that early dismissal would take place at 11:00 a.m. Following the announcement, my classroom phone rang numerous times with requests for students to leave with a parent. Students who had been waiting all morning to leave and go home sprang into action to clean up the art supplies.

Stepping outside the school building, I felt dazed and disoriented. In complete silence, my colleagues and I made our way to the faculty parking lot. Along with a shared slow deliberate walk to our cars, there were a few nods and waves. When I finally got into my car to leave, I took a few deep breaths. I had spent the day trying to contain my emotions in order to protect my students. Within the privacy of my own car, I let the pent-up tears flow. After I calmed down with a few more deep breaths, I headed to my mother's house to unite with my daughter. While I still didn't know about the safety of my ex-husband and his brother, I continued to pray and hope for the best.

Being reunited with my daughter and mother was medicine for my soul. Marissa and I held on tight to one another.

"I'm so sorry I couldn't get to you sooner," I said.

"Mom, I am so worried about Dad and Uncle Steve."

Although I shared the same feelings, I struggled to find a way to comfort her. "I know Hon, I've been thinking of them all day. Let's remember that they have many other job sites in the city. They may not have been at the World Trade Center. All we can do is pray and hope for the best."

We were trapped together in a surrealistic nightmare. Watching a lone news reporter at an empty John F. Kennedy Airport felt unreal. Normally, sitting outside on the deck with my family on a beautiful starry night would be a joyful experience. The absence of airplanes in the now silent sky above us was an eerie and unsettling reminder of what we were going through.

We received a message from one of my ex-husband's colleagues who assured us that he and his brother had not been at the Number 5 World Trade Center site and that they were safe. Within the next few days, all the buildings at the World Trade Center complex collapsed into ruin. Communication and travel to New York City had officially come to a halt. It would take a week before we could actually speak to my ex-husband.

When we returned to school, the students banded together for fundraisers and food drives to assist first responders and survivors. Everyone adorned their vehicles with American flags or patriotic ribbons. Zach, a graffiti artist, asked if he and a group of his fellow students could create a mural in the school building as a tribute to September 11th. Since the sketch of the artwork was done in his graffiti style, he was concerned that the school would not accept it. When I brought it to the principal, he gladly approved the design.

I spent many late afternoons painting with my students to create an amazing 30' by 40' mural in the high school. The process of creating the mural was a healing outlet for those who worked on it. It became a powerful emotional symbol of remembrance for our community.

Despite the construction of the Freedom Tower in 2006, my beautiful Emerald City skyline will never look the same without the Twin Towers. The loss of the skyline symbolized much greater loss; the loss of life and the loss of feeling safe.

Collective grief still resides with such artifacts, shared stories and memories of the events of 9/11. Every year on the anniversary of September 11th, two huge columns of light rise up from Ground Zero to touch the heavens. It remains an appropriate tribute and representation of our collective grief, community and resilience.

The depth of despair, that I thought I managed rather well, was triggered while watching an episode of Northern Exposure, in which New York City was referred to as The "Jeweled City of the North." As the Manhattan skyline complete with the Twin Towers came into view, my tears poured forth as if a dam had burst. In that pivotal moment, I made a commitment to myself to learn how to navigate my pain.

I found new ways to use my heartache as a catalyst for alchemy. I intensified my yoga practice by including highly spiritual Kundalini yoga. My creative pursuits of journaling, creative writing and therapeutic neurographic art facilitated my healing journey. As I created new art pieces and short stories, these methods successfully integrated my past trauma, while allowing me to step into the future.

I've come to realize that humanity, much like the Chiaroscuro technique in art, is defined by the coexistence of bright light and deep shadows. Despite the darkness of the tragic terrorist attacks on September 11th, the light of love, compassion and service continued to shine through. This contrast resides within each one of us. We each have the power to create our own unique composition. We can choose to dwell in a world of shadows, or we can choose to live in the light. Just like turning on a light in a dark room, the light always overcomes the dark.

"Namaste," the familiar salutation used in yoga practice, translates to "The light in me honors the light in you." I believe that the more people acknowledge the light in one another, the more we can come together to utilize Chiaroscuro as a way to create a beautiful collective masterpiece.

About Lorraine Manzo

Lorraine Manzo is an author, award-winning educator and artist based in New York. Her short stories have been featured in popular publications including *Dan's Papers* and *ACES Magazine*.

Lorraine is passionate about exploring the connection of body, mind and spirit through her multidisciplinary work. She utilizes her extensive experience as an artist and educator to develop empowering public workshops that incorporate the therapeutic benefits of writing, guided meditation, yoga and neurographic art.

Website: www.lorrainemanzoart.com

Lorraine's gift to you: Healing Neurographic Art Workshop

Visit: https://linktr.ee/lorrainemanzoart

Wisdom from the Womb: Sacred Choices of Motherhood

Chapter 8

THE ARRIVAL
HOW MY SON'S BRIEF YET POWERFUL VISIT OPENED MY HEART AND AWAKENED THE DIVINE WITHIN

Emilce P. Suarez-Lipton, LCSW

I lay on my bed on a rainy day, feeling like I had run for hours with no destination. Surrendering to grief, I allowed my tears to match the rainfall and prayed for my sadness to be washed away. The last fertility treatment had failed, dashing my hope of having a second child.

A sudden realization interrupted my tears: My period is late! "What if I am pregnant?" My heart's dim light brightened as I rushed to the bathroom to take a pregnancy test. Could I have gotten pregnant naturally? My hopeful, yet skeptical mind spun while I waited for the results. Then, "Pregnant" appeared on the stick and I felt my heart jump! I took another test and "Pregnant" appeared once more. The glowing eight letters shouted out at my skeptical self, "Yes! You are pregnant!" My heart's dim light exploded into fireworks.

My joy grew as the weeks passed. At eleven weeks, my husband, Noah, and I went in for a test to assess markers of genetic problems. I was nervous, but mostly excited for my sonogram. Bloodwork had shown that we were expecting a boy, so I was eager to see my baby boy. Things were going well until suddenly, everything shifted.

"There seems to be a problem," my doctor said with a sharp, tense voice. He proceeded to tell us that the sonogram showed markers for a very serious genetic disorder. I immediately burst into tears.

Noah held my hand while trying to stay calm. "What kind of disorder?" he asked.

The doctor addressed Noah's questions, but no words that came from his mouth indicated a chance of hope. The room became foggy ~ my body was there, but the rest of me was not. "What is happening?" a part of me whispered, but there was no response. One moment, I was bubbling with joy; the next, my doctor alluded to the interruption of my pregnancy.

After agonizing days waiting for results from further testing, it was confirmed that our son had Trisomy 13 and would likely not make it to birth. The best, yet unlikely, scenario was that he would be born alive but would die soon thereafter. My heart's fireworks turned into a slow-paced cracking of a crystal vessel; although not fully broken yet, cracks formed one after another, announcing the crystal's destiny.

As the floor beneath my feet also began to crack, I prayed for a miracle. However, upon doing extensive research about the diagnosis, we learned that our son would not stay with us. The more Noah and I talked about how to proceed, the clearer it became that we wanted to allow the pregnancy to take its course. There was a part of us that thought our baby might be the exception, born with profound challenges and yet capable of living. "This may be our last chance, so I want to prolong this experience for as long as I can, even if it will be extremely short-lived," Noah said with calming clarity. He also suggested that we name our son. We named him Fabián Richard in honor of Noah's uncle, Richie.

The decision to let the pregnancy continue was difficult for some to understand. Sherry, my mother-in-law, was very loving and supportive, yet she struggled to embrace Fabián, anticipating the inevitable outcome. However, by the end of the second trimester, she asked if she could join one of the prenatal appointments to see the baby. I appreciated her openness.

Several years later, Sherry shared with me an essay that she wrote about Fabián's visit. She wrote: "I choose to support the baby's parents, to let them know that I love them even more, and want to share in caring for what they care about. So, I too will embrace him while he is alive, not knowing if I will ever be able to hold him in my arms." I am still deeply moved by her acceptance driven by love.

Our daughter Juliana's response to the news about Fabián's prognosis is ingrained in my heart. "I am sad that the baby is sick, but I am glad that Mommy is fine... if she is fine I'm okay," her wisdom belying her nine-year-old body. Our family moved through this challenging experience with grace and love. We wanted Juliana to have as much normalcy as possible, so we traveled, went to concerts, and we had our usual fun lives. But we also held space for each other as we navigated the waves of fear and anticipated grief.

~~~~~~

Fabián was born on a beautiful summer day. I loved my sweet angel's plump cheeks and full hairline. Sadly, we did not get to see his eyes open, yet we felt his beautiful presence. When I held his warm, tender body in my arms for the first time, I felt I knew this loving being whom I had fallen in love with since the day I became aware of his visit.

My son was surrounded by family as he transitioned from this reality only 23 hours after birth. Gathered at the hospital, we

~ his grandparents, his uncle, and his aunt ~ held him, sang to him and spoke to him. Sherry sang a Yiddish lullaby to Fabián, introducing herself as his bubba. We all held him tenderly and loved him. The unwavering support from family and close friends sustained me through the challenging bereavement.

Fabián's visit, however brief, opened my heart at different levels. Initially, it was a joy opening through the miracle of a natural pregnancy. Seven months later, I had to say goodbye to Fabián and move through unbearable loss, which was the most challenging experience I had ever faced. This level of heart opening was devastating grief that cracked me open. The purifying fire of grief melted my broken heart, yet it eventually transformed me from the depths of my soul.

~~~~~~~

Four years after Fabián's visit, my private practice was thriving and everything was going well, but the void that Fabián left still showed up like a crushing wave of debilitating sadness.

I longed for connection to my son. I would often sit on my bed and open his memory box. As tears rolled down my cheeks, I sought confirmation that he had been here. I gazed at his pictures. I held his blanket, traced his footprints with my fingers, and as I clutched the birth card with weight, length and date of birth, I realized: All of it was evidence that Fabián existed. "You were here and I held you in my arms. I sniffed your head and cradled your soft, precious body," I would say to him with an exhale.

I searched for the same tenderness that I felt when I passed my fingers through my daughter's hair when she was a baby. Eyes closed, I imagined caressing Fabián's velvety cheeks and smooth curls. For a brief moment, I found connection to him through these fantasies and let my love for him flow. Despite the rawness of grief, my love for him was always met with a comforting, warm embrace. I swaddled Fabián and he swaddled me back.

Eventually, I felt called to journey inward and mend my heart. The void in my womb mirrored a void in my heart that I had no idea how to fill. I reached out to my friend Hilda, who graciously had offered me multiple Reiki sessions while Fabián was in utero. She also performed Reiki on him at the hospital. In a beautiful speech that Hilda wrote for Fabián's memorial, she mentioned that when she blessed him, Fabián moved suddenly, "...as if the force of all our love and energy had traveled through him. I believe that he received our blessings and was enveloped in the warmth of our love." Hilda thanked me for welcoming her blessing of Fabián before he transitioned. I feel that Fabián blessed her as well. Through Fabián, my friendship with Hilda blossomed. I was incredibly grateful for her generosity and loving presence.

I told Hilda I was seeking more than just healing my grief. "There is more to Fabián's powerful visit that I still can't figure out after four years," my voice cracked.

Hilda took a deep breath and let me cry. Then she replied: "I feel like you and Noah navigated this painful process with such grace and courage, and for a loss such as this, grief can take a while to process."

I took a deep breath, appreciating Hilda's validation.

Her next question forged the course of the rest of my journey. "Have you ever consulted a psychic?"

"I have only consulted Tarot readers a few times," I replied skeptically, "but nothing meaningful came out during those experiences."

"Well, not long ago, I felt like I needed spiritual guidance in making a decision, so I contacted Ahriah, a psychic recommended by a friend. The experience was unlike any other. It was weird, yet very helpful."

As Hilda shared in depth about her experience with Ahriah, I felt a door opening in my heart. It sounded "woo woo," but also intriguing. I trusted Hilda and the feeling in my heart that was guiding me to explore this.

Ahirah encouraged me to practice meditation. She taught me that channeling was a form of meditative practice that aims to connect to higher frequencies within the depths of the heart ~ "the seat of the soul," she would say. This marked the beginning of a wild ride into my heart's world. As a psychotherapist, I was aware of my psychological world. My heart's, and more specifically, my soul's world, felt unfamiliar, yet I was drawn to it.

I felt called to experiential courses on breathwork, meditation, mindfulness, and channeling. I consistently practiced what I was learning, and messages came through as epiphanies and vivid dreams. Nevertheless, I still yearned for a more palpable channeling of my soul and my soul's guides because I felt like that would fill the void left by my son.

One night after my bedtime meditation, I asked Fabián for a sign of his presence. "I do not want to be scared," I said with a smile. That night, I woke up around 5 a.m., and when I opened my eyes, I saw six circles of bright white light on the left wall right above my altar. They looked like lights reflecting from the window, except my blinds and blackout curtains were completely shut. I got up and opened the curtains to see if there was something outside my window. There was nothing. I closed the curtains and blinds and sat on my bed, stunned!

I looked around the room, trying to make sense of what I was seeing.

After a while I realized that I could not explain it. Thus, I just stayed there, staring at the bright circles with conflicting feelings of disbelief and astonishment. As I gazed at them, I began to feel a sense of presence in the room... a familiar, loving presence. Somehow, I knew that there were multiple energies present and that Fabián's loving embrace was one of them. "I am here. I love you," this energy said. I felt expansive and floaty, but sharply awake.

Soon after, a warm vibration and buzzing moved up and down my body like gentle waves of electricity. I considered waking Noah, but hesitated, wanting to focus on enjoying this magical moment. I smiled with gratitude as I placed one hand on my chest and said, "Thank you." I lay down and closed my eyes, but kept opening them every now and then to check if the circles were still there. They shone brilliantly until I fell into a deep sleep.

The next night I experienced the same visit. As soon as I woke up hours later, I drew what I had seen both times, and realized that the shape created by the bright white circles of light resembled the letter Y. It made me think of a constellation, but also reminded me of a chalice. "What does this mean?" I wondered. The circles of light showed up on my wall for several nights around the same time. They returned a few more times over the next two years, until I no longer needed a physical sign of Divine presence.

During meditation, one week after the initial arrival of the lights, I received another special visit. As the energy in the room softened, a woman glowing with translucent blue light appeared in my mind's eye. I heard "Sagrado Corazon" (Sacred Heart), followed by "Re-read my gospel." This message reminded me of Magdalene. A golden chalice came to mind.

Intrigued by my unique visitors, I searched online for the gospel of Magdalene and its esoteric interpretations. The idea that stood out: Divinity is within us, not outside of us. "Sagrado Corazon" came through during meditation after these visits, as an invitation to bring my awareness to my sagrado corazon, the portal to my soul. Placing one hand on my chest, I breathed deeply, visualizing my heart opening like a blooming flower. "Expand, expand, expand," I said aloud as the image of my heart's glowing light expanded to fill my body, and eventually the entire room. Immersed, I enjoyed the peace within.

After months of consistent practice, I was guided to speak whatever came through during meditative states. The more I allowed, the more it flowed. The more it flowed, the more I trusted my sacred heart's expression.

One day during channeling, I asked my soul about my current period being unusually painful. I heard, "Source takes different forms," and an image of a chalice with overflowing blood came to mind.

"This appears gross to you because you are associating this blood with something bad. Consider the chalice representing your heart space filled with Source energy. When you arrive at your sacred heart you experience the cosmos within and you see the blood as Divine."

As this message came through, the blood inside the chalice became a beautiful flow of nourishment and vitality. With my eyes closed and feeling the flow of energy, I saw the blood moving through my veins and arteries. My pounding pulse felt like a powerful force. "I am alive, I feel the beat of my consciousness," I said with a smile on my face... and the image of blood transformed into an overflow of bright red roses.

As I took a deep breath in gratitude for these visions, images came to my mind of women in my family, myself included, that had chronic issues with their reproductive organs. Feeling compassion for our bodies' pain, I took another deep breath in honor of our endurance and strength. "We lived, we released, we co-created," my sacred heart said. I realized that I was shedding energies I had held in my womb for my mother and her mother. My perspective on my painful period shifted.

With time, my journeys into the depths of my sacred heart revealed increasingly deeper levels of awareness. I looked forward to this intimacy with Self, welcoming shifts in perspective and the reclamation of my power.

About a year later, I felt guided to sit in ceremony with "Mama Cacao." I had experienced beautiful healings and fascinating journeys with San Pedro, a very gentle psychedelic plant medicine. But I wanted to sit in ceremony with a non-psychedelic plant. Well, Cacao arrived and she never left.

This loving plant brought the most important medicine I have received: True Love for Self. I dove deeper than ever into my heart to get to know and embrace myself as a multidimensional being. Cacao supported me through another level of heart opening. This one I call, "Remembrance." As I lit my candle and played my singing bowl preparing sacred space for my daily Cacao ceremony, I felt an arrival home. "I did this before," my sacred heart said. Images came to me as chanting would flow from my lips. I saw myself burning herbs in a community temple and under the full moon's light. I sat in circles with women as we communed with the light within us and that united us.

In Ceremony with Mother Earth and the Cosmos we rejoiced. "It's coming back to me," I whispered, moved by the homecoming feeling.

"Embrace in love, with love, and for love all the parts of you," I heard my heart say. "Even the ones you consciously or unconsciously put in exile, even the aspects from unknown worlds and dimensions. You are ready to receive more of you into your sacred heart." My heart became my home I came back to every day.

One Friday afternoon, I was deep in meditation when spontaneous sounds began to emerge: "Achamacuchuna amaya." Soon after, I felt like I wanted to move my hands. I brought my right hand to my chest, then hovering it, I traced the sound coming from my heart up to my throat and then out through my lips. I sounded out these nonsensical syllables as they flowed through me while my hands moved.

And then, something amazing happened! I got into a rhythm and Light Language began to flow faster and faster: "Acuyamayaendara-kataia-urrkurtishkitiara-acayamanaca-taya...ereketearakata-isha-ukienaeta."

Language of Light is a multidimensional transmission of frequency that bypasses the human mind and penetrates multiple levels of the body, supporting healing and integration. I had seen a few channelers speak Light Language online. I found it weird yet intriguing, and very relaxing. However, I never thought I would be able to speak Light Language myself.

After an hour my sore throat continued allowing sounds to emerge. It felt like parts of me that had lain dormant for a long time awakened and had a lot to say. Noticing heat that concentrated in my core that then moved to the rest of my body, my rolling tongue moved faster. The tone of my voice shifted. I giggled, then laughed.

The fireworks in my heart returned. "Rejoice," "Liberation," my soul exclaimed. It was a family reunion with different aspects of myself: ancestral, galactic, angelic and elemental energies ~ all in my heart. It was invigorating. In between short breaks to allow my body to recover and catch my breath, I felt a loving vibration moving through me. I spoke Light Language for about one and a half hours.

Since then, I speak Light Language every day during my own meditation and channeling, as well as during sessions and Cacao ceremonies with clients. "Speak more like that, please," some of them say with eyes closed and smiles on their faces. Often, they experience visions as they receive the frequency of the Light Language.

The activation of my Light Language profoundly supported the integration of all the work I have done since Fabián's visit. I call this level of heart opening "Arrival." I no longer see the divine inner wisdom as one part of me. It is me. I AM the divine multidimensional consciousness that runs through all that is me.

~~~~~~~

It has been nine years since that rainy day when I yearned for the arrival of my second child. My son Fabián came for a brief visit that precipitated an unexpected journey of multilayered heart openings. Intrigued by my ethereal visitors, I longed for a palpable spiritual connection to Fabián, because I thought that would fill the void that he left. Through seeking him, I realized that there was a deeper void within me. I had been seeking out rather than in.

Therefore, I was guided to dive deeper and deeper into my sacred heart and allow myself to sit with the grief, the longing, and other younger parts of me that needed healing. With the support of beautiful, aligned energy healers and mentors I met along the way, I allowed myself to be in this unfolding. This fascinating journey led me to my own arrival.

Emilce P. Suarez-Lipton

Even though I am still a human that, at times, experiences grief and self-doubt, I am now sovereign, and I trust, co-create and express myself in a more whole way. This arrival completely shifted the way I work with clients. It gives me the greatest joy to hold sacred space for them, so that they, too, open their sacred hearts, and arrive at their divine truth and wholeness.

Fabián continues to have a presence in our lives.
His photo and footprints grace our altars.
He visits us often and keeps company
with others that we have lost.
Juliana, now 18 years old, loves her brother,
and sees him as the family's angel.
I felt his presence and guidance all
throughout writing this chapter.
Thank you my sweet angel.

ABOUT EMILCE P. SUAREZ-LIPTON, LCSW

Emilce P. Suarez-Lipton, LCSW, is an Intuitive Psychotherapist, Energy Healing Facilitator and Conscious Channeler who is passionate about supporting people with their healing, Self-embodiment and awakening journey.

After fourteen successful years in the mental health field, Emilce experienced a heart Awakening. This initiated a fascinating journey to the embodiment of her multidimensionality and true love for Self. Mind-body-spirit practices including meditation, energy work, channeling and plant medicine ceremony supported the emergence of Emilce's intuitive gifts. She then felt called to integrate these gifts and practices into her work with clients.

In addition to psychotherapy, Emilce offers energy healing, conscious channeling and Light Language transmissions. Light Language is a non-linear form of communication and channeled, multidimensional frequencies of sound and light, that facilitate healing and inner trust. It is Emilce's greatest joy to hold sacred space for others so that they also know, love and trust themselves.

Emilce loves nature walks, dancing, Yoga, meditation with Cacao, and spending quality time with her husband, daughter and their sweet dog, Alvin.

Website: www.emilcesuarezlipton.com

Instagram: heart_openings_activations

Blog: Heart Opening Activations at www.emilcesuarezlipton.com

YouTube: https://www.youtube.com/@heart_opening_activations

Chapter 9

SACRED CHOICES:
SOULFUL CONVERSATIONS ON INCARNATION

Julie Norman, BS, E-RYT/YACEP, CDCA

"She's mine."

The words hung heavy in the autumn air between us. My voice was strong and clear again. I met his once intimidating gaze with fierce courage, a feeling I'd forgotten. Myla, the sweet brown dog who had shared his torment, stood steady at my side. In this pivotal moment, his attempt to keep her only strengthened my resolve to reclaim the vital part of me that I had surrendered.

Without another word, I opened the door to the tiny car crammed full of everything I owned. Myla eagerly jumped in. I looked around one last time at the shimmering water, stately trees and yellowing meadow grass. I had, just a few months earlier, roamed that land around our meager apartment, waiting for wisdom to arrive. I bowed my head in gratitude before wiggling in behind the wheel and driving off without the slightest glance back.

~~~~~~

I was dancing the day we met, my body pulsating to every beat the band played. Friends and I were celebrating the life of a young friend who had died unexpectedly. She would have wanted us to be dancing. He walked in as her favorite song started. Our eyes met and we smiled simultaneously. There was a boyish innocence about him. We flirted back and forth as I rocked out to "Mustang

Sally." He looked on in awe. I could tell he'd never seen a woman so free, so alive, so comfortable in her skin... especially one that challenged the culture's thin ideal with her curvy, fluid edges.

I was used to surprising others this way since recovering from my eating disorder a few years prior. To this day, people often assume I'm drinking, or even drugged, when shamelessly singing karaoke or dancing with reckless abandon.

My friends are often asked, "What's her deal?"

They proudly report, "She's high on life!"

I fought hard for that freedom. Nothing matters more to me than belonging to myself. This is my wish for every soul on earth, especially women.

As our group left the venue that day, my admirer followed us out into the summer sun. He watched me cross the road and boldly climb on the back of a friend's Harley-Davidson. I shot him one last look and winked. He smiled sheepishly, then looked down, nervously shuffling his feet. It was so freaking adorable that I waved him over and we exchanged numbers.

Cody called later that night.

Our courtship was fast and furious. Reflecting back, I was highly vulnerable at the time. While my recovery was solid, the rest of my life wasn't. I'd recently made massive changes, from dropping out of grad school and starting my own business, to breaking up with "Mr. Perfect" and quitting my decade long equestrian career. To top it off, I was grieving my friend and healing from nearly having my throat ripped out in a terrifying dog attack. I had resolved my painful body image and eating issues, but was struggling to find my way into the next chapter.

Cody was cute, charming and loved the outdoors. We had childhood heartbreaks in common: both our fathers struggled with alcohol and our mothers with mood disorders. He shared so openly about his own challenges and newfound sobriety that I assumed he was all good. He made me feel special and convinced me that working on himself ~ a strong value of mine ~ was a priority. He was enamored with my story, my friends, and even my dreams. From the pickup truck I drove, to my career goals and love of horses, he embraced it all with open arms and promised to support whatever my heart desired.

I would later learn this was trauma-bonding and love bombing, common dynamics of unhealthy relationships. That was just the beginning. Three months later we eloped in Vegas. Though he promised it wouldn't be an issue, Cody started drinking the minute we landed in Sin City. I told myself it was an exception and surely he'd stop once back home. He didn't. As an adult child of an alcoholic, I reacted the only way I knew how. I squelched my emotions and needs to "help" him feel better, and thereby stop his drinking. Sensing my vulnerability at that time, he convinced me to move an hour away from my family, friends, and career; a common strategy for abusers.

Cody's early infatuation with my authenticity morphed into a trigger that resulted in near constant ridicule. The strong, yet soft, body I had worked so hard to reclaim was now a target. I was still healing her from diet culture and years of restriction, bingeing and purging (compulsive exercise, laxative abuse and self-induced vomiting). Porn became an added element. He wanted me to watch and imitate it with him. I refused. Next, his spending spiraled out of control. In response to the chaos, I started cutting corners wherever possible. I took on boring long-term care consulting instead of building my nutrition therapy practice. Because we'd stopped having sex, I went off birth control to save a whopping thirty bucks a month. Having been on it for eleven years, I figured getting pregnant was highly unlikely.

I encouraged therapy, but finances were his cop out. Ashamed of the situation, I kept it all to myself. Luckily, our landlord was an astute and kind man. He could see we were struggling, and offered us free training in transcendental meditation. Cody only went to the first class, but I continued. This was before my yoga journey, but I sensed it was an immense gift ~ one that Cody was unwilling, or perhaps unable to receive for himself.

Six months into the marriage, I moved into a separate bedroom. I was mindful to make it my own with soft colors, a meditation spot and equine imagery. It was my safe space until the night Cody came home drunk after the second shift. Rather than passing out on the couch as usual, he barged in as I slept. For years, I blocked out what happened next. I knew we had sex but that it was different, very different. I knew I tried to stop it. I knew it was wrong; very, very wrong.

What I *do* remember vividly was waking up alone at dawn to the most magical light shining through the tiny cinder-block window. I lay there for the longest time, watching the dust dance in its hazy rays. I felt disconnected from my body and heavy-hearted, my mind racing to fight back reality. Suddenly I felt a warm, all-encompassing presence and a confusing moment of peace. Then the shrill ring of the phone jolted me out of bed. My mom wept through the line, stuttering, "He's gone." Her father, my precious PaPa, had passed. My shock took precedence over reckoning with what had transpired just hours before.

Being with my family for the funeral stabilized Cody. Perhaps the reminder that I had outside support gave him pause. He promised things would be better, and I believed it. A few weeks later the smell of coffee suddenly made me nauseous. Because I adore coffee, my first thought was, *"Dear God! Something is horribly wrong!"* My intuition nudged me to take a pregnancy test which, sure enough, was positive.

"Well shit..." was my initial reaction.

Cody, on the other hand, seemed strangely pleased. When I shared that I didn't know what I was going to do about it, he snarked, "What do you mean *you* don't know?"

I asserted, "Exactly what I said. *I* don't know what *I'm* going to do." This threw him for a loop, my having power beyond his control. I requested we keep the pregnancy private until I decided. Instead, he intentionally told my mom, which further complicated things.

I was strongly considering abortion. I had never planned on having kids, mainly because I'm a true-blue tree hugger. I figured I would foster or adopt should motherhood beckon. Add my toxic relationship to the mix and the choice *seemed* obvious, yet it didn't feel so clear. I decided to "sit" with my experience, something I'd learned through recovery, and more recently, meditation training. This proved quite challenging. My mind, my husband and my mom *hated* it, but my heart held my feet to the fire. I had to let go of trying to figure it out, making endless pro/con lists, and trying to think my way to an answer. I became increasingly comfortable in the unknowing. Something told me to simply trust and clarity would arrive in divine timing.

Cody and my mom could hardly bear the waiting. To their near constant inquiries, I'd simply state, "I don't know." This came to feel like a prayer. Gloria Steinem's quote, "The truth will set you free but first it will piss you off," often came to mind. Through this process of wise waiting, things began shifting within. It felt increasingly safer to soften and surrender ~ to stop seeking, doing, questioning ~ and just be in the messy mystery. Reflecting back now, I have great respect for that version of me. I'm so fucking proud of her. What a wild and wonderful way to love myself.

One oddly warm winter day, I went for a long walk. Just me and Myla, the dog Cody had acquired for hunting. The one who, despite her pedigree and training, defied his commands. The steady pace of our squishy steps lulled my mind ever more into the moment. Suddenly I received a message, "*I want to come.*" I stopped dead in my tracks.

Without question I looked up to the steely sky and responded, "Are you sure? It's really hard down here."

They said yes.

I'm not sure how long I stood there immersed in the gravity of what transpired. Until then, I'd only considered the pregnancy as something that would keep me stuck. My perspective abruptly shifted. Part of me now felt sure I could do this alone if I had to, or simply if I wanted to. Realistically, I knew Cody's demons weren't going any-where anytime soon. I'd watched my own father war with those same demons my whole life. It was the root cause of my eating disorder. Regardless, I gave Cody the benefit of the doubt and stayed. He didn't change, but I did. As my belly grew, so did my resilience, which was met with more and more narcissistic abuse. Luckily, my pregnant form repulsed him, likely an aversion to the fullness of the feminine: that which he feared most in himself.

Though my family and friends were far away, we had moved Patrick, my retired show horse, to a barn nearby. I made daily trips to care for him, and enjoyed trail rides well into my third trimester. I cherished those moments with Patrick; he knew me better than any human ever will. Our connection was integral to my recovery. I often joke that he was my first yoga teacher because he taught me self-love, emotional intelligence, what karma really means, and more. He was the manifestation of my pegasus-obsessed childhood dreams, and was now passing that magic on to the soul inhabiting my womb. Had I not learned to embrace my body as a consort, a conduit for divinity, I would have never heard their desire to join us earth-side.

On Sept. 11, 2001, I went to the barn early. It was one of those exquisite weather days and I felt sad I couldn't ride given I was now seven months pregnant. Strangely, our landlord was there when I returned. He looked unusually unsettled. He asked if I had seen the news.

"Nope." I said. "Why?"

Without a word he led me into the apartment where the TV blared. He pointed to it and said, "World War III just started."

I turned away after only a glimpse of the burning towers. I didn't want that terror to access my womb. I left without a word, hustled back to the barn to tack up my horse, and climbed clumsily into the saddle. Patrick carried us carefully into the woods, where I wept and prayed for peace.

The very next day I left Cody. Nine-eleven had illuminated the terror I was allowing in my own life. I moved into a beautiful historic home with a generous lesbian couple my sister knew well. They lived just a mile from the hospital, and halfway between work and my hometown. It was a perfect space. They prepared a gorgeous lavender room for us with white crown molding and tall windows that reached the floor. It had a stunning antique wardrobe with a huge mirror. I'd stand in front of it naked, reveling in the magnificence of my body, ripe with nascent life.

Ally arrived a month later. To say I was over the moon would be an understatement; I was absolutely enchanted. Although part of me did worry about developing postpartum depression given the impending divorce and my family's mental health history, that was not the case at all. Every morning, I would check in with myself, and then shrug, "Nope. Still freaking happy!"

I started a special journal for Ally. It had a rainbow and two dolphins on it, symbolizing our unique journey together. I wrote in it daily that first year, noting everything that was happening in our lives: the joys and the pain, my hopes and dreams, and the divine feminine wisdom I wanted to pass on. I kept that up over the years, less consistently of course, but I filled several journals. For Ally's sixteenth birthday, we went to the Big Island of Hawaii. I gifted her the journals by the Queen's Bath in the Kalahuipua'a Fishponds.

Shortly after her birth, Ally and I moved to a cozy, one bedroom apartment back in my hometown. Sadly, the drama with Cody continued. He reverted to love bombing and begged for reconciliation. Suddenly, he was all about therapy and returned to AA. I had zero interest. I was back in my power, with my people, and deeply committed to giving my daughter the best life possible. Ironically, that was also my Achilles' heel. Despite knowing deep down he'd never change, it broke my heart to imagine Ally fatherless because of my own wounds. Although my own dad had been physically present and a great provider, alcohol kept him from showing up fully for his family, which left me with a hefty abandonment wound.

Cody moved back in with his family, including his dad, a Vietnam vet with PTSD who was kind but short tempered. Since he was sober himself, I hoped he could help Cody get his shit together. However, their relationship was volatile at best. Most concerning was Cody's older brother with untreated schizophrenia, who also drank. Cody told me his brother had molested him when they were kids, and as adults they often got in full on fist fights. Shockingly, none of this was of concern to the broken family court system we were now embroiled in. I was encouraged to send this young child there for unsupervised visits, which, thankfully, Cody didn't pursue that first year. He could see Ally anytime at my mom's house, but rarely did, and instead developed the narrative that I was "keeping his child from him." (Abusers often center themselves as the victims, rather than taking responsibility for their behavior.)

Ally was barely two months old when I started working full-time. I had to. Child support was a joke that barely covered a week of groceries. Luckily, I landed a position as lead dietitian at a psychiatric hospital that had just opened an eating disorders program. I bought our first home soon after. That's when Cody began insisting Ally go to his place for visits. I refused. He threatened to call the cops, to which I responded, "Go ahead. Over my dead body will I send them there." A guardian ad litem got involved and co-parenting classes were mandated, but were unhelpful. Cody could work any room to his favor. In desperation, and fearing the worst, I abandoned myself and re-entered a relationship with him so that I could stay overnight to protect Ally during his visitation time.

It felt like I was living a double life: one in my beautiful new home surrounded by family and friends, with steady work; and one where I had to succumb to the control of someone's else's pain. However, I stayed diligent with my meditations, and had found my way onto the path of yoga. This bolstered my resilience through it all, but despite using protection the few times we were intimate again, I "mysteriously" got pregnant once more.

This time was much different. I knew not to suffer by seeking a decision, but rather to surrender and listen for the voice of the soul making contact. I kept the pregnancy private to keep the channel clear. I slowed down, deepened my healing practices and waited with surprising ease. One day, while meditating in the tiny third bedroom I'd painted a dusty purple hue, the message arrived.

"I'll stay back," they whispered. A tear rolled down my left cheek. They continued, "But I'll always be with you." I replied through more tears,

"Thank you Gia. I love you." That name had been in my consciousness for years. In fact, I was surprised I hadn't given it to Ally. Now I knew why.

One wintery Ohio weekend, my best friend came to stay while I braved a medicinal abortion in the comfort of my own home. My antique clawfoot bathtub and steadfast sisterhood held me tenderly through the waves of painful cramping and primal grief. Throughout it all, Gia reassured me of their choice and surrounded me with amazing grace. When I passed the blood clot they left behind, I wrapped it in tissue and gently placed it in a silvery teal, gold and rose silk pouch that once accompanied a gorgeous sarong I had gifted myself before marrying Cody. Many moons later, I buried the pouch on sacred ground: somewhere very special to Ally, Patrick and me. The matching sarong now adorns every altar I create for my women's circles, workshops and retreats.

The Cody issues continued. Both Ally and I gave him countless chances to change, but disappointment and heartache were the only outcomes. Ultimately, Ally made yet another sacred choice to emancipate herself from him completely, the details of which are her story to tell. Through it all, I've felt Gia's unwavering compassion and cosmic guidance.

Despite all the pain with Cody, I still believed in love and found it again. First, with Dale, who was a steady and lighthearted force in our lives through Ally's early years. Then, finally, with Dave, my beloved husband whom I married on September 11, 2015, and who Ally rightfully calls Dad because he shows up for her the way a father should. On September 14, 2024, we walked her down the aisle together to her own true love.

Every day, I'm grateful for my messy and magnificent life, especially my journey to body peace, and how it empowers me to navigate uniquely feminine challenges such as these. Had

I still been battling my body, I would never have been able to connect with and engage in sacred conversations with these incredible souls. I believe it is vital for each and every one of us to support each other as we heal from all things that disconnect us from Source ~ our innate divinity. I believe this healing work is essential to dismantle the archaic patriarchal, misogynistic, white supremacist systems that are destroying this earth and stripping away fundamental human rights.

Furthermore, the soulful conversations that guided my decisions solidified my pro-choice values, reframing choice as: a deeply personal dialogue with those who might manifest through me. To be honest, I ignorantly took my right to choose for granted back then. I never imagined we'd be in the horrific *Handmaid's Tale* reality that is unfolding here in the United States in 2025. We all need to be having sacred conversations with friends, family, community members and political leaders to return and uphold reproductive rights. The sacred feminine in all of us, despite body dimensions or gender constructs, is the portal through which love is born again and again.

ABOUT JULIE NORMAN, BS, E-RYT/YACEP, CDCA

As the creator of *Body Karma Healing: Change Your Body Image, Change The World,* Julie has guided thousands to reclaim their lives from food, weight and movement challenges that limit health, happiness and full creative potential.

Julie's extensive work in eating and substance use disorders programs as both a registered dietitian and trauma-informed yoga instructor, plus her 30 years of personal recovery enables her to serve clients with confidence, compassion and creativity. Her services are weight-inclusive and HAES (Health At Every Size)-based to support the whole person: body, mind and soul.

She offers coaching, workshops, international retreats, consulting and speaking. Julie loves to travel, write poetry, mountain bike and be with her beloved family, friends and animals.

Free Gift! *Sacred Embodiment: Prose & Practices for Feminine Empowerment*

Contact: julie@julienormanyoga.com

From Darkness to Recovery

Chapter 10

PROTECTION OF THE GODDESS ~
HOW MY SOUL GIFTS PULLED ME OUT OF A CHASM OF GRIEF AND SHAME

Rachel Chase MA, BFA, CYT

When I hit rock-bottom in 2002, I was lying on my living room floor, faced with a choice offered by voices in my head.

It wasn't the first time my spirit guardians spoke to me.

MYSTICAL MEMORY

I am a toddler sitting in a stroller. My parents and I are relaxing at a neighborhood park near our home in southern California. People are all around ~ families smiling, children playing. The grass is vibrant green and gigantic shade trees reach skyward all around us.

Suddenly, golden light is radiating from everything and everyone! I feel bigger than my body. What a delightful expansion. I'm not thinking like a child. A greater consciousness merges with my young mind. More than a vision, this is a fully embodied experience of union.

A loving, feminine voice in my mind urges me to remember what I see and feel in this moment.

"*Don't forget. Remember. Remember.*" she urges, beckoning.

I am transported into a vision of light that weaves the Universe together. This light courses through my body. My elevated state lingers for a few minutes. Then I return to normal.

No one else seems to notice what just happened.

I now believe the golden light I saw that day was a visible expression of living consciousness that dwells within our body-mind-energy system, what yogis call *kundalini*. It is the undying sacred light of love that lives in all of us. The blessing of that gift left a powerful imprint, a compass to guide me through the darkness of my grief and shame.

CRASH LANDING

I stumble out of my car, drunk out of my mind. The cop is saying, "You need to come with me now, Rachel." I whirl around to see the pickup truck I've just smashed into.

"*I ran the red light. Shit! I ran the red light. NO!*" I yell to myself.

I suddenly remember: karaoke after my bartending shift with the owners of the bar. "*Damn.*" Tequila shots, at least four. Singing on the mic, wild and free. Walking straight out the front door. The bouncers didn't stop me. Getting in my car. The owners of the bar didn't stop me. Driving away. No one stopped me... until I crashed.

It was the late '90s in Tallahassee, Florida. Those were hot days, running far from the demons of my grief. Pushing hard on overdrive. No signs of relief.

Until... life delivered a few heaping doses of strong medicine to stop my self-destruction.

Unbreakable Spirit

I'm on my living room floor, frozen, struggling to wake up from an evening catnap. I can't move my face. My body weighs a ton. I hear myself gasp a little. Somewhere in the distance, voices: "*Move, Rachel! Wake up, Rachel!*" Body won't move. I groan. I could slip away and die. "*What?! No, no I don't want to do that. I want to wake up!*" I'm all alone. What if no one finds me? I struggle to find consciousness. A magnetic slumber pulls me down. I'm in the liminal space. There's a presence in my mind. Voices from another dimension, "*It's up to you. You can leave now, or stay and find your purpose.*"

It takes a minute to comprehend this choice. I strain to wake up. Then I jolt awake with a start. Instant denial. The intensity fades quickly. I tell myself it wasn't as bad as it seemed. Another snooze button on life's alarm clock.

After a shower, I go out to the club to dance it off.

Ecstasy was my club drug of choice. I was queen of the dance floor, unleashing my inner whirling dervish 'til the break of dawn. Fly little bird, fly! Consequences be damned! The last laughs were mine for the taking. Until the next alarm… and the next….

Time's up! Final wakeup call.

After seven years of overuse, my 27-year-old body burns out. Dehydrated. Undernourished. Run down. Opportunity knocks. I am awake but can't move the left side of my body.

"*Wait, I just laid down for an afternoon nap!? Oh my god, what's happening to me?*"

By the end of the day, I can move but I feel stiff and foggy. Doctor says it could be MS or a stroke. Clearly the MRI scans show a swelling in my brain.

"This isn't real, is it?"

What I wouldn't give for a cigarette. Or a drink. Vices numb the shame.

EXPLOITED

My shame was a tricky monster, rooted in spiritual abuse from birth. It grew stronger after complex grief and sexual assault in my twenties. I hid my true feelings in a cloud of denial that drained my power, leaving me listless and weak. Although painful and humiliating, those crises led me to find my purpose. I have since learned how to clear toxic energy, heal my wounded heart, and find my true self. The journey has been a rocky path on which I have stumbled, parched, starving for magic and reaching for grace.

I was born and raised in a bible cult called The Way. Our charming, maniacal leader, Dr. Victor Paul Wierwille, dominated the lives of tens of thousands around the world in the 1970s and '80s. He was an authoritative father-figure with all the answers. I remember him up on stage, gripping the front of his podium, shouting in his country preacher's voice.

My parents, like the rest of his followers, worked full time to please him and get the "Word over the World." That was the mission. Two vulnerable seekers, easily conned by the promise of having "Power for Abundant Living." They were in their early twenties when they met in The Way's new leadership program, got married soon after, and had me a few years later, in 1975. We moved constantly, sometimes living with other ministry families in California and Florida. We hosted weekly fellowships in our homes, and knocked on doors to recruit new members. Blind agents for a madman's vision.

From 1984 to 1987 we live near The Way's headquarters in the little country town of New Knoxville, Ohio. As part of the ministry's elaborate performances, I get to dance and sing for our congregation on Sundays in our huge auditorium. I also get well trained in the art of being a good girl. If I follow the program, I might avoid getting possessed by "devil spirits" like the non-believers, or getting punished if I do not live according to "The Word." Whatever that meant.

Insidious messages like these made no sense to me. But I kept my confusion to myself. Suppress and smile. It kept the peace. People-pleasing meant safety, albeit tenuous. It has taken many years of deep self-reflection and compassion to dismantle this coping mechanism.

I tried the best I could to feel okay even though I wasn't. In fact... everything was falling apart.

"Set the table, honey." A familiar dinner time directive from Mom. Lips pursed. Furrowed brow. The obvious look of concern. I don't ask questions. If the table is set right, we are picture-perfect. Nothing to see here. I watch my dad, once the free-love hippie, contort to fit into his minister's façade. He is cracking under pressure.

My parents' pain breaks my heart. Although they love me unconditionally, they yell at each other all the time. I cry in bed at night sometimes, anxious and sad. I don't want to be a burden, so I hide my anxiety behind a cheerful mask.

Life is not all bad. I have lots of friends. We ride bikes after school, splash in the creek, and play "Spin-the-Bottle" in the corn fields. Streets are safe for us latchkey townies. One day after school, my friends and their older brothers come over. We are a wild bunch of ten and thirteen-year-olds. The boys dig out my dad's porno mags and VHS tapes from his not-so-secret hiding places. I climb up to the top shelf of the liquor cabinet and snag whatever is up there. Down in the musty basement, we play pool and drinking games like "Quarters." Who needs supervision, anyway?

Dad works in The Way's warehouse, a demotion for his rebellious streak. That's what happens when you challenge Dr. Weirwille's authority. Mom works in the research office where she starts to notice discrepancies and cover-ups. People are getting fired for questioning protocols. By our second year in Ohio, she has discovered the scheme.

A shockwave hits our family. We've been pawns in a liar's game of sexual abuse, plagiarism, false promises, greed, and mind control.

Dr. Weirwille's death in 1985 is followed by a brutal fight for the ministry's leadership. Powerful men from the inner circle maneuver to inherit his lucrative international empire.

We try to act normal while Mom and Dad covertly plan our way out. The three of us flee Ohio. We abandon everything and head down to Central Florida, far from the drama of a community in chaos.

ABANDONED

I am swept up in a hopeless storm and hurled into a huge suburban middle school. Nothing means anything anymore, not even God.

I rescind respect for my parents. How am I supposed to believe what they tell me now? Time to conform to a new set of rules? Screw that. I get sent home for wearing a short miniskirt on the first day of seventh grade.

My parents' marriage implodes over the next three years. Out with a bang. Now it is just Mom and me. Life has been intense for so long, now it feels boring.

Puberty starts and I am on the hunt to find a boyfriend that will have sex with me. Hungry for attention and desperately wanting to be wanted. Burning with anger on the inside, good girl on the outside. I excel in school. Don't want to worry Mom.

I throw myself into the life of a semi-professional dancer, practically living at the studio for five years. My refuge and solace, dance connects me to my true self. When I am performing, life has meaning and purpose. I get to shine my heart-light on stage and share it with the audience.

It was a good enough escape for a while. But then it wasn't. I quit dancing for my company at sixteen, right after a successful recital and competition season. The pressure for perfection was too much.

I was sick of trying to be good all the time. *"Who am I? What am I?"* Desperation thrust me into self-destruction. Drinking parties on weekends. Sleeping with steady boyfriends and other boys in between commitments. Grasping to soothe the lost place inside me.

After high school, I am living on my own, bartending, dancing professionally in night clubs and theme parks, and partying a lot. Then, I'm molested and raped on separate occasions by guys I thought I could trust. *"I was drunk, what did I expect? They couldn't help it after all,"* I thought. I continue stumbling downhill with what little self-worth I have left.

Then, I fell in love, hard. Bryan had potential, a sharp creative mind. He wanted to be an architect. He loved me intensely and exposed me to a drug-laden underworld that felt exciting. I left my job: dancing in the same show every day, 4 times a day, at SeaWorld. My buddies helped move me out of the city to a new life with Bryan on the outskirts of town.

Bryan and I lived together for 3 years. Madly in love, we tested the boundaries of consciousness together, experimenting with various psychedelic drugs. We were reaching for the sublime in a world of pain. Misunderstood and misdiagnosed, I wanted to save him from his manic depression. Our romance was a ticking time bomb.

We can't escape our demons forever.

One afternoon, I walk into our bedroom and find Bryan frozen on the bed, his skin slightly blue. Screaming, "Bryan!" and jumping on his body, I pound my fists on his chest. Sobbing in desperation, I drag him into a cold shower. Lying wet in my arms, he snaps out of near-death. Who knows what he took too much of that day.

For the next few months, I am torn between staying and saving my own life. I even find myself staring in the bedroom mirror one day, pointing a loaded gun at my head.

"What am I doing?!"

I wanted to save him. But who would save me? My soul urges me, *"It's time to go."* Devastated, I move out to live with friends. Then, several weeks later, I get the call that he's dead.

Two weeks before that call, he had driven his motorcycle over to my place. I can see it like it was yesterday.

I open the door and watch him slowly walk to my front door, helmet under one arm. Such a sad look on his face. My heart drops. I let him in. I ache to see him. I want to go back to him. Sitting next to me on the couch, holding my shaking hand, he tells me how much he wants me back, how he can change. Crying, trying to steady myself, I channel my strength.

"I wish I could. But I just can't. The pain of loving you is too much."

Slumped in defeat, he walks out the door.

A week later, the call. "Uh, hi Rachel. Last night some of us were partying at Bryan's place. We tried to wake him up this morning. He went too far. I think he meant to. The ambulance just took him away. I'm so sorry, Rachel."

I want to die. "*It's all my fault!*" Panicked thoughts overtake me. "*How could I have done this to him? I should have given him another chance!*" I blame myself entirely for his death.

Devastation swallows me whole. I swim deep into the numbing well by smoking copious amounts of cannabis and using antipsychotic pills to escape the pain. Heavy with grief, I don't get out of bed much.

Two years later, I find myself in emergency surgery for an ectopic pregnancy. My boyfriend turns out to be violent and abusive. More grief and shame. I jump from relationship to relationship. All the while, the voice of my soul pleads, "*You are meant for so much more than constant turmoil.*" I yell at God on a regular basis. "But that's all I've ever known! How am I supposed to change my life when it's always been this way?!"

I attempt to stay in college, but drop out each time I lose interest. I feel like a failure.

My drinking is out of control.

A few more dark years go by before that day I hit rock-bottom, lying frozen on my living room floor.

RECONNECTION

It took a few months to regain full mobility after that final wakeup call when I was 27. Rays of hope mingled with dark days. Scared straight, I stopped drinking, smoking, and taking drugs for one year. No easy task.

For seven more years I worked as a head bartender. A wild scene... late nights, fast cash. Rocky relationships continued. Undoing the habits of self-abandonment and substance abuse takes time.

I believed in the possibility that I could heal my body through the mind-body connection. I just had not quite understood how yet. My harsh, judgmental self-talk stood squarely in the way of navigating through the darkness.

"*How could you be so stupid,*" my inner mantra taunted me daily. Fifteen years of being angry at God had nearly closed my connection with divine love.

"*When will life get easier?!*"

On my knees, I cried out to the Universe in agony. "*HELP ME!*"

I soon found out She was listening.

"Reiki? What's that?" I ask my new friend. I am standing by the back door after teaching a dance class at a local senior center. We are on our way out when I confide in her, "I still have nerve pain, weakness, and vision problems. I feel stuck and stupid, like I've taken too many wrong turns."

She gives me a tender look of empathy, then offers to give me something called Reiki. "It's a gentle form of healing touch," she explains.

I cry a little at the sound of something so pure.

"Yes, please, that sounds wonderful," I tell her.

She gently places her palms on my shoulders. Energy pulses through my body immediately. A big release of tension. I feel much lighter. I need this.

The following weekend, she introduces me to her teacher, Gary. He teaches me how to use meditation, visualization, breathing, and my own hands to heal myself. During group classes, we explore self-healing topics like relationship boundaries and self-compassion. This is all new to me. I'm allowed to have boundaries with people? Never mind forgiveness. That daunting process feels like an arduous hike up Mt. Olympus.

"Be patient but persistent with your healing process, Rachel," Gary would say. "You are learning how to shift your emotions. It takes time and practice to learn new ways of being."

The more I meditated, the more connected I felt. I saw visions of rivers of light flowing from the cosmos into my body. I could hear reassuring voices of divine guidance and feel a powerful force of love all around me. The fortress of protection around my heart and mind began to dissolve and I started to feel safe in the world again. Reiki became my gateway to living in alignment with my higher purpose.

Slowly, the new life I was destined to create begins. I learn about traditional healing through Chinese medicine from my acupuncture doctor. Then I take a sound healing course and attend ecstatic dance workshops. As a dancer, yoga feels natural, so I sign up for a yoga teacher training program. Then, I follow my bliss to a fine art degree at university. My creative spirit awakens again. Reiki, meditation, art making, and yoga practice help me find my intuition and trust in myself. Now I can be adventurous in a grounded way. Now I can see and follow the Universe's clues on a path to wholeness.

Writing, dancing, music, printmaking, and video art helped me make sense of my past, process trauma and express my deepest feelings. Creative expression transformed pain into power.

My soul gifts blossomed as I learned how to express my true self. Glimmers of excitement turned into shimmers of possibility.

I could taste the sweetness of my future dreams coming true.

DIVINE DESTINY

It's the summer of 2005. I'm dancing barefoot in Venice Beach, hips swaying to live drums, the ocean air thick with salt and rhythm. I lose myself ~ then find Her. The Goddess inside me rises, radiant and fierce. "*I am You,*" she whispers. Under moonlight that night, I wade into the Pacific, heart wide open, remembering something ancient. I embody Her essence deep inside, "*You are the goddess.*"

One year later, in a quiet LA lobby, I see a flyer glowing like a sign from the Universe:

"**Retreat to Unconditional Love ~ Maui.** With Ram Dass, Jai Uttal, Michael Beckwith, and Mark Whitwell ~ December 2007."

"*Yes, please!*" I'm totally there. All I want to do is heal and get my life on track. Maybe I'll find what I need in the presence of these amazing teachers.

In Maui, everything hums ~ frangipani breezes, sacred chants, the pull of soul family. On the third day, I slip into the back of the retreat meeting room.

Ram Dass speaks slowly: "God is..." His eyes lock with mine. Stillness. A soft quake inside me. I close my eyes and see waves of sound flowing into infinity. I make a silent pact to live my life in service to Divine Love.

Tears well in my eyes as I surrender in relief to the path made known.

That night, Jai's kirtan music swells. I rise, singing and spinning in devotion. Ram Dass, dancing in his wheelchair next to me, beams his huge smile and waves his arms in the air. I become Durga, the goddess of protection ~ wild, holy, unstoppable. My eight arms slice through illusion. I remember who I am: a goddess of love and courage.

In the 18 years since, I have cultivated my soul purpose as a teacher, creative, healer, and guide on the path of love. Using the power of self-compassion, I've healed and grown beyond what I could have imagined. No longer lost, I live an intentional life. I get to help others heal as I continue to heal too.

And I get to grow alongside the man I love. We met in Maui during the retreat and married two years later. Together, we are learning just how true it is that love is the healer.

About Rachel Chase, MA, BFA, CYT

Rachel Chase writes to honor the unstoppable human spirit and to heal the wounds of the heart. Creative expression is her lifeline ~ a way to alchemize grief, speak the unspeakable, and find her way back to the truth of who she is.

Through her healing and coaching practice, she helps others heal and live with purpose. Her teachings, circles, and transformational programs invite women to return home to themselves ~ to live, love, and lead from the truth of who they are.

At the core of her offerings is the belief that compassion is the medicine that softens the armor around the wounded heart, allowing the true self to breathe, bloom, and be boldly expressed in the world.

Download her *Healing with Self-Compassion* book here:
www.freecompassionbook.com
Visit her website: www.rachelchase.com
Email: rachel@rachelchase.com

Chapter 11

MY SACRED REBELLION ~
A STORY OF LOSS, LIGHT, AND LEGACY

Michele Campbell,
Sacred Rebel Healer

There are moments in life that change everything ~ where reality splits into "before" and "after." For me, those moments didn't come just once; they came in waves, each one breaking me down before building me into the healer I am today.

As a child, I always knew I was different. I was deeply sensitive, intuitive, and aware of things I couldn't explain. I could sense emotions before they were spoken, feel the pain of others as if it were my own, and I knew things I wasn't supposed to know. It was as if I was plugged into a higher frequency that no one around me seemed to understand. Instead of feeling gifted, I felt burdened. I didn't understand how I was able to pick up on the secrets, emotions, and pains of others without them ever saying a word. The adults around me were unaware of my struggles, and because I couldn't explain my experiences, I internalized them. I carried the weight of emotions that weren't mine, convinced that something was wrong with me.

Looking back, the first time I remember feeling the undeniable power of my gift, I was with my father. One morning, as I watched him getting ready for work, I couldn't shake this immense feeling of fear. I begged him not to go, clinging to him, pleading with everything in me. I didn't have the words to explain why ~ I just felt something terrible was going to happen.

He brushed it off, assuring me that everything would be fine as he walked out the door.

That day, a man entered the building where his office was and opened fire on the people inside. When he came home, shaken but unharmed, he didn't embrace me or acknowledge the fact that my fears that morning had been valid. Instead, he warned me not to tell anyone what I had done, as if the way I had felt that morning was something to be ashamed of. That was the moment the doors to my gift slammed shut. If the very thing that had tried to protect him made me different, made me *wrong*, then it was safer to silence it.

My confusion about all the things I had been experiencing turned into anger. I became rebellious, misunderstood, and desperate to escape. By high school, I had already found my way to drinking, using meth, and basically doing anything that I could to dull the intensity of what I had been feeling. It wasn't just about getting high, it was about silencing the knowing, numbing the loneliness of feeling different. If I couldn't belong, at least I could disappear.

For years, addiction became my refuge. The more I buried my gifts, the more I craved an escape. But when I got married and had kids, I forced myself to stop using. I told myself I was done. But even though the drugs were gone, the need to numb never left. Instead, it shifted ~ to food or shopping. On weekends, I drank and took pills, searching for new ways to blur the edges of reality. Even when I built a new life, becoming a massage therapist, I was still carrying the secret. The knowing. And it was too much.

Years later, after my divorce, I found myself alone with two small children, standing at a crossroads. I had spent so much of my life feeling lost, but I knew I had to figure out who I was ~ not just for me, but for them. That's when I enrolled at the National Holistic Institute and became a massage therapist and health educator.

It felt like a fresh start, a chance to rebuild and create a stable life. What I didn't expect was how this path would awaken something buried deep within me.

As I began working with private clients, my gifts came back full force. I would see spirits around them. I would know things about them ~ things they had never told me, things even they had forgotten. The floodgates had opened, and my knowing was no longer something I could ignore.

But I still carried my father's shame. His warning all those years ago echoed in my mind, convincing me that there was something wrong with me. So, I kept it to myself. I never told a single person what I saw, what I felt, what I knew. I worked in silence, pretending that what was happening wasn't real. But the more I ignored it, the stronger it became, until eventually it became impossible to deny who I really was.

And yet, I still wasn't fully connected to my true self. I was hiding from my gifts, running from the truth, and struggling to make ends meet. That's when I fell into an abusive relationship. I had my youngest son while trying to maintain my massage practice and a home, all while enduring the pain of that abuse. When I finally found the courage to leave and get a restraining order, I was still left to figure things out on my own. I had no choice but to find a way to survive ~ to keep a roof over our heads, and to keep my massage business going.

But the shame of what I had to do to make ends meet only deepened my need to escape. I drank more. And then came the drugs. What had once been an occasional relief became a daily habit, numbing me from the pain, the struggle, and the truths I wasn't yet ready to face.

And with the drugs came something else ~ an awareness I couldn't turn off. I was picking up on spirits, energies, and presences that clung to the house I lived in. Shadows flickered in the corners of my vision; whispers brushed against my ears. Emotions that were not my own settled into my chest like a weight I couldn't shake. I didn't understand it. I didn't trust it.

Later in life, I researched the land and discovered that my home had been built over an old network of underground tunnels, likely used during Prohibition for smuggling and secrecy. Yet, as I stood in that space, I could feel a deep echo of forgotten stories and unspoken fears lingering in the walls, the floors, and in the very air I breathed. It was as if the pain and secrecy of those who once passed through had left an imprint, a residue that whispered through time. I was living inside a story that had never been fully laid to rest.

But at the time, I didn't know what to do with it. It was all too much to handle.

And then there was Charla, a Native American friend who often came over. She was the first person who truly saw me ~ the first person who made me feel that what I was experiencing wasn't just in my head. Charla would sit with me for hours, listening with an open heart as I described the energies I felt, the spirits I saw, and the messages that came through. And she never doubted me.

She would nod, her bright eyes filled with understanding, and tell me, "Yes, they are here. You're hearing them. You're seeing them. You have a gift."

And for the first time, I believed it. I could describe her ancestors to her ~ their clothing, their faces, the way they stood watching over her. I could hear them, feel their presence, and Charla's unwavering trust in me gave me the confidence to trust myself. She was the first person to reflect back to me the truth that I had been too afraid to accept.

I am so grateful for her. But even with her validation, I wasn't ready to step into my power. I was still running ~ from my pain, from my past, from myself.

So I ran. Again. Into addiction. Into silence. Into the only escape I knew.

THE SPIRAL INTO DARKNESS

Losing my children shattered something inside me. It wasn't just grief ~ it was annihilation. One moment, I was their mother, clinging to the last threads of stability, and the next, they were gone ~ taken by my own family. My home, my business, and everything I'd built slipped away. I had no reason left to keep fighting.

I cried out for help, but the world seemed deaf. I felt invisible, as though my pain was too much for others to witness. I began numbing the unbearable with alcohol and drugs. What started as an attempt to quiet the screams became my only reality. The days and nights blurred. I lost everything.

I didn't sleep on sidewalks. I survived in another world ~ one that seemed glamorous from the outside. I played a role, wore a mask. It was illegal, dangerous, and addictive. For a time, it felt powerful. The money, the attention, and the chaos fed my desire to forget who I was.

But I was drowning. The shame pressed down on me like a weight I couldn't shake. I had to drink just to exist in the persona I'd created.

And then, it all came to a screeching halt. I crashed in a stolen car I didn't know was stolen. The world flipped. I almost lost my hand ~ and nearly my life.

I woke up in the hospital, nine surgeries ahead of me, barely stitched together. That year in recovery was agony ~ physically, emotionally, spiritually. I was trapped in a broken body and a haunted mind. At first, I was furious. Was this punishment? Was God condemning me?

In the silence, something deeper stirred. The voice I'd buried as a child began to whisper. I wasn't being punished ~ I was being called back. This was a reckoning. I had survived for a reason.

But instead of rising, I fell again.

After the hospital, I was placed in a room in San Francisco's Tenderloin district ~ a place thick with despair. It took just a week to relapse. The isolation and filth around me mirrored what I felt inside. I spiraled deeper.

That's when I met him. A towering man, intense and magnetic. He was more than just another addiction ~ he was a karmic mirror. Our souls had met before. His power pulled me in, but it was rooted in shadow.

Even though his presence was toxic, I stayed. I mistook intensity for love, and danger for protection. He became the next layer of my descent.

Then, breast cancer. Stage three.

Even before the diagnosis, we had been running ~ city to city, chasing survival. When I received the news, I was staying with my uncle. I had the surgery, but after the hospital discharged me, I had nowhere to go. I was denied treatment because I was homeless.

We fled to Las Vegas, hoping for care. There, they treated me regardless of housing status. At first, we lived in a van. Eventually, we found a place ~ but the chaos didn't end. My uncle drank. My partner used. I was caught between their destruction and my illness.

I began chemo, thinking it would save me. Instead, it almost killed me. My spirit was disintegrating. I was hospitalized again, barely holding on.

Then, in the stillness of that hospital room, I heard it:

"You don't have to fight. You have to listen."

I remembered. My training as a massage therapist and health educator. I had known the body was sacred. That knowing returned.

I stopped fighting and started healing.

I began turning inward, guided by an inner knowing that I could no longer ignore. I returned to natural medicine, drawn to the wisdom of the earth and the teachings of Dr. Sebi. I embraced detoxification, alkalized and plant-based nutrition, herbal healing, meditation, and energy work. Slowly, my body began to restore itself. My immune system strengthened. My spirit began to stir. The fog started to lift.

I wasn't just surviving anymore ~ I was remembering.

I made the difficult but necessary choice to release the relationship that had become misaligned with my healing. It wasn't about blame ~ it was about choosing life, choosing peace, choosing myself.

A dear friend opened her home to me in California. I arrived bald, wrapped in scarves, but breathing freely for the first time in years.

That moment marked the beginning of my sacred rebellion ~ against every story that said I was broken, unworthy, or beyond repair. I reclaimed my health. I reclaimed my voice. I reclaimed the power that had always lived inside me.

And then, the most devastating loss came.

My daughter Violet ~ my light, my reason ~ was killed in a car accident.

Just months before, we had been making plans. She had visited me in the hospital in Las Vegas, wrapping her arms around my battle-worn body as if nothing had changed. We talked about her moving in, starting over together. I saw hope in her eyes. I held on to that vision like oxygen. That dream ~ our dream ~ was gone in an instant.

The moment I got the call, I remember collapsing to the floor. It was as if the world cracked open beneath me and swallowed me whole. My body convulsed with a scream that wasn't even human ~ it came from the deepest, most primitive place in my soul. A sound carved out by lifetimes. In that moment, a part of me died ~ the part that only existed because she did.

The grief didn't just break me ~ it erased me.

I wandered through days and nights like a ghost. I couldn't breathe, couldn't eat, couldn't pray. My heart didn't just ache ~ it collapsed. Every breath felt like betrayal. How could I continue when she could not?

I relapsed almost immediately. All the healing, all the work, all the light I had fought so hard to reclaim disappeared. I reached for anything to numb the pain. Substances dulled it for a moment, but the sorrow always came roaring back ~ louder, sharper, more unbearable. I was drowning, and I didn't want to be saved.

None of the spiritual tools I'd gathered felt strong enough to hold me. I questioned everything ~ my purpose, my path, my very existence. I screamed at the heavens. I cursed the Divine. I told Spirit to leave me alone. I didn't want signs. I didn't want comfort. I wanted my daughter.

But even in that darkness, whispers came.

They didn't sound like words at first ~ more like threads of energy brushing against my spirit. Violet. My father. My ancestors. I could feel them on the edge of my consciousness, holding vigil for me when I had abandoned myself.

At first, I shut them out. I told them to go away. I wasn't ready to heal. I wasn't ready to rise. I wanted to disappear.

But Violet's love never left.

She showed up in dreams, her eyes glowing with the same fierce light I'd always known. I saw her in the flicker of candles, in butterflies landing on my arm, and in the exact song we once sang together playing at the gas station at midnight. Her spirit was everywhere, reminding me that love never dies.

Eventually, I surrendered ~ not to life, not to healing ~ but to the truth that she was still with me. That her soul had become a guide, not just for me, but for the work I was meant to do in the world.

And then, one year after Violet's death, my father passed.

His death closed a chapter that had shaped much of my silence. My father was a man who carried his own unspoken wounds, and he taught me ~ intentionally or not ~ that seeking help was weakness. In our family, we didn't talk about mental health. Vulnerability was dangerous. Therapy was for people who couldn't handle life. I was told to stay quiet, to hold it in, to toughen up ~ because any sign of weakness could and would be used against me.

But when he left this world, something inside me shifted. It was as if the chains I didn't even realize I'd been dragging finally broke. For the first time, I gave myself permission to ask for help ~ not because I was weak, but because I was finally ready to be free.

His death became the doorway to my healing.

The timing wasn't lost on me. Two of my lineage, ancestor and descendant, both leaving within a cycle of grief and rebirth. His departure deepened my ache, but it also clarified the call: it was time to rise. Not for them. Not even for me. But for the legacy of healing that they had passed into my hands.

Their love ~ especially Violet's ~ became my lighthouse. Her absence ignited the next phase of my awakening.

Because her love never left... and neither did mine.

Grief cracked me open. I googled "holistic rehab," and was led ~ by divine force ~ to Hemet Valley Recovery Center.

There, I met Sherry Burditt, the director and author of *The Gift of Addiction*. She showed me that my pain wasn't punishment. It was sacred. It was purpose.

She introduced me to the chakras, to soul contracts, and to ancestral healing. I realized I had chosen these experiences before I was born ~ to evolve my soul and heal my lineage.

I was never the black sheep. I was the healer.

Everything shifted.

I left Hemet not just sober, but spiritually reborn. I understood who I was ~ and why I had endured it all.

From that point forward, I devoted myself to understanding trauma, energy, and the subconscious mind. I enrolled at Hypnosis Motivation Institute (HMI) and became a Clinical Hypnotherapist, mastering neuro-linguistic programming (NLP) and subconscious reprogramming. I graduated with honors.

But something deeper still called. I joined Rose Cole's Shamanic Academy, now Sacred Oak Academy. There, I reawakened gifts that had always lived within me.

I remembered how to walk between worlds ~ both physical and spiritual. I trained in mediumship, learned to work with ancestors and spirit guides, and embraced energy healing as my native tongue.

Sound, frequency, and vibration became sacred tools in my practice. Rituals became acts of creation. I studied Past Life Regression with Dolores Cannon and explored Jungian shadow work, realizing healing *must* be multidimensional ~ body, mind, soul, and lineage.

I became a Clinical Hypnotherapist and Spiritual Counselor at Passages Malibu, supporting clients on their journeys of recovery, self-worth, and spiritual awakening.

I rebuilt my relationship with Violet in spirit. She's now one of my greatest guides ~ her presence lives in whispers, in the wind, in the soft glow of synchronicities that appear when I need them most. She walks with me every day, guiding my steps as I walk the path we dreamed of creating together.

In connecting with her, I also began connecting with my ancestors ~ those who endured lifetimes of hardship, silence, and survival. I feel their presence with me now, no longer as shadows of the past, but as wise and willing allies. Their strength flows through my veins. The healing I do now stretches backward through generations and forward through time.

But this healing didn't stop with the unseen ~ it extended into the heart of my living family.

For the first time in my life, I began rebuilding relationships with my bloodline. With tenderness and boundaries, I started showing up differently. I softened into compassion for the wounds we've all carried ~ generational trauma, unspoken pain, codependency, addiction, secrecy. I no longer saw myself as separate from my family ~ I saw myself as the bridge.

I became the one who initiated healing.

Through conversations, rituals, and energy work, I began weaving repair into our dynamic. I didn't wait for them to be ready ~ I simply *became* the healing and let it ripple outward. And slowly, they began to shift too. We laughed more. We shared more. We listened deeper.

I've become a better mother to my sons. Not just present ~ but awakened. As I healed the mother-daughter wound within myself, I opened space to love my boys with more presence, grace, and emotional integrity. I teach them the work I do. I teach them how to breathe through pain, how to name their emotions, how to honor their intuition. I teach them how to return to themselves.

And it doesn't stop with them. My extended family has become curious about what I do. I've led energy healings for my relatives. I've helped them release grief, anxiety, and ancestral burdens they didn't have words for. I've watched my healing become a mirror for their own.

I am not just transforming myself. I am transforming my lineage.

The Sacred Rebel in me doesn't fight my family ~ I love them into their remembering.

All of this has led me to my soul's work.

I founded **Sacred Rebel Healer** ~ a sanctuary for transformation. I guide clients through hypnotherapy, Guided Energy Medicine™, past life healing, and energetic reclamation. My mission is to help others awaken their sacred rebel ~ their power, their truth, their sovereignty.

I now understand that every descent I lived through was an initiation.

Every trauma was a teacher. Every collapse, a portal.

I was never broken. I was always becoming.

And now, I walk in my purpose.

Not as a victim.

Not as a survivor.

But as a Sacred Rebel.

ABOUT MICHELE CAMPBELL
~ SACRED REBEL HEALER

Michele Campbell is a Clinical Hypnotherapist, Guided Energy Medicine™ Practitioner, and Intuitive Healer specializing in trauma, addiction, and soul transformation. Her own journey through addiction, a near-fatal accident, breast cancer, and the loss of her daughter awakened her purpose as a healer.

Michele is trained in Clinical Hypnotherapy, Shamanic Healing, and Past Life Regression. She is the founder of Sacred Rebel Healer, where she blends hypnosis, energy medicine, and spiritual activation to guide others into deep healing and personal power.

Her mission is to help others break free from limitations, reclaim their truth, and remember who they truly are.

Learn more at:

www.SacredRebelHealer.com

linktr.ee/Sacredrebelhealer

Scan the QR Code to be connected to your free gift.

Burnout and Reclamation

Chapter 12

STEPPING AWAY FROM THE LEDGE,
COMING HOME TO MY SELF

Aimee Tomczak, MA, LMFT

As I closed the brown wooden door of the shingled condominium that she had bought after divorcing my father 25 years prior, I knew my mother was crossing a threshold and would never return. I remember walking behind, her beloved cream white poncho sweater wrapped around her frail shoulders. The slow *click - click - click* of her metal walker, tapping an unsteady rhythm on the brick path towards my waiting car. We were taking her to an Assisted Living facility. It was time, as we could no longer care for her in the ways she needed. After several mini strokes and falls, she had been diagnosed with Alzheimer's dementia, which would mean a painful and fraught journey for all of us.

My shoulders were tense, my chest tight from hardly breathing. The achy lump in my throat kept any feelings down. This was just too hard. *"Stay moving, get her in the car,"* I told myself. My mom was always good at pretending everything was fine. We both knew how to do this act well. This was the last time she would walk past the potted plants, pink rose bushes and doors of Nancy and Charlotte, neighbors who had become wonderful friends. She was leaving the home she had claimed after ending the tumultuous relationship with my father. The home she decorated how she wanted: full of colorful Mexican animal figurines and vibrant art. I felt like I was holding the grief for both of us. She was losing herself and I was losing her.

My grief felt like some far-off land that my heart could not travel to. My lifelong vow to make sure she was okay was being tested. I struggled to hold this new reality and my own deeper pain of decades of putting her needs ahead of mine. My heart could not travel there, as I feared I would be swept up and washed away by a massive ocean of grief.

Maintaining control of everything related to her care and her needs had been my goal. If I could just be a good enough daughter and manage everything, including my feelings, then it would all be okay. Growing up, both of my parents had mental illnesses. The chaotic mood swings of my bipolar father plus mom's anxiety and depression engulfed our house. Their relationship was filled with conflict and verbal abuse. When my mother was pregnant with me, my father abandoned us and moved back to his hometown in Illinois. She had very little support, so I was molded from my earliest years to be her emotional caregiver. My father returned to us about a year and a half later, but I had already taken on the role of being the "good daughter" as a survival strategy to stabilize my fragile mother. My father molested my little sister and me in the shower multiple times as young girls. No one protected us. I felt responsible for my sister and took on the role of caretaking her. As a little girl, I made a vow to make sure my mom was okay. This survival strategy worked for years, but at an enormous cost.

I was in my late forties, and over the years I had pushed many parts of myself down. The expressive, creative and passionate parts of me, the wild parts of me. I hadn't created art just for the pleasure of it for almost 20 years. It was easy to wear the constricting mask of the good daughter and good worker. I could fit myself into whatever shape was needed. That strategy had worked well for a long time, but now it was crumbling. My romantic relationship of nine years was ending. Things with my partner had become strained due to the amount of time and energy I was expending attending to my mother's declining health and needs. The end of that relationship was painful. My authentic self was slowly being drained and I was out of touch with the full spectrum of my emotions. With the intensity of my perimenopausal hormonal shifts, I was haunted - wondering if my life was becoming a mirror reflection of my mother's.

As a young woman, my mother was very intelligent and had dreams of becoming a creative writer or a lawyer. However, the high school guidance counselor told her she only had two options: to become a teacher or a nurse. Communication in her family was so poor that her parents didn't let her know they couldn't afford the plane fare from California to Pennsylvania, which meant the full scholarship she was awarded to attend Bryn Mawr college would not be hers. This was a heartbreaking hijack of her potential.

In 2016 I was working as a Psychotherapist in community mental health. My job in the treatment program was: group therapist for people with chronic and persistent mental illness. I loved the work, but the bureaucracy was worse than the actual job. I was doing the same job as I had as a child. I didn't realize the unforeseen crisis awaiting me as my mother's health declined and I faced menopause.

I was absolutely exhausted, anxious, sleep deprived and on an emotional rollercoaster. I was dragging myself around with no energy for the creative endeavors that I had loved: dancing, writing, painting. I was not even journaling. I was totally cut off from the juiciness of my own Soul. I knew how to show up for Mom ~ dutifully doing what needed to be done, but I was depleted and numb. The scary part was that it felt like I could just keep going like this. I was getting used to a life that was flat, dissatisfying and devoid of meaning, with no color, juiciness, or spark.

My mom passed away in March of 2018. In her last months, she was in hospice in a long, slow dying process. I stalwartly stayed by her side. As her body began to shut down, her swallow reflexes became weaker. At one point the nurse said we need to clean out her mouth. She was no longer eating solid food, so I didn't understand what the accumulated gunk was, but that cleaning was horrible to witness. The nurse used a special swab and was pulling out lots of yucky gunk. Instead of allowing myself to feel the horror of seeing this, I became more vigilant and felt a need to make sure the nurse was doing it "right."

Even after my mother had stopped drinking water, she lived for another nine days. The hospice nurses told me how unusual this was. She just kept hanging on. As the dutiful daughter, I came back day after day to her bedside. Being stalwart kept my feelings of grief at bay. This was a very difficult vigil because my sister had broken down with exhaustion and I didn't have an intimate partner for support. It was excruciating and exhausting.

My grief after she died in 2018 was immense. It felt like a seismic shift that split me open and dropped me into an unknown abyss. I had no idea who I was anymore. All I knew was raw anger, sadness, and pure exhaustion. I missed her and my familiar identity as her caretaker. I was angry that I had been neglecting myself for decades and hadn't been able to set better boundaries. I was angry that it felt like I was the only one who could do what needed to be done. I was angry that I had sacrificed so much of my life for my mother.

I felt unmoored. There was deep grief under the anger. While I loved her and would miss her, I also felt relief that she was finally gone. As I fully allowed myself to feel the grief, a new spaciousness began to emerge, slowly and gently, inside my body, heart and mind.

It took about a year before I could start to reconnect with myself and ask: *"Who am I now and what do I want?"*

I bought a condo, my first ever home. While it was exciting to have my own place in the city, deep down I ached for my true desire to live in the green, peaceful countryside with more nature around me.

Connecting to my desires and longings was really uncomfortable at first. Anxiety, as well as anger, continued in my transformative process. It was so hard to listen to my needs and claim what I wanted. I tried to do things I thought were "right." What I didn't know was that these things that seemed "right" weren't what my well-being and spirit were calling for. What I didn't know was that the lessons of this time would be very difficult ~ yet would guide me to finally listen to my heart's true longing.

What I didn't know was that in the next two years, upon moving into my new condo, I would hire a contractor to paint and replace baseboards and find black mold in the walls. What I didn't know was that I would be fighting with my HOA and insurance company for my right to have my living expenses covered, and the mold remediated. What I didn't know was that after all of that, there would be a flood in my condo, which would leave me displaced, living in a hotel room for six months. All of this happened at the beginning of the COVID lockdown.

My mother was now gone, but it seemed so hard to find and create a safe home space. I felt victimized and beaten down as one thing after another went wrong. Because I was still working as a therapist in community mental health, I was at higher risk for contracting COVID. So my friends and family weren't comfortable having me stay with them, for fear of exposure. I had no choice but to stay in a hotel with my cat, Pumpkin, for months on end, while the world was in pandemic lockdown.

I remember one late afternoon, I returned to my hotel room, exhausted from my therapist job at the clinic. It was another depressing evening in 2020, as I stared at the dull gray and brown couch and worn striped carpeting. Looking out my 8th floor hotel window with its sliding glass doors and cold, vertical, grey metal bars on the balcony, hopelessness took over. In the distance I could see the San Francisco Bay sky with an orange and pink sunset, but all I felt was pure exhaustion and a burning resentment that this was all happening to me. A heavy despair pressed further into my chest.

I just wanted to give up.

I began to contemplate taking my own life. My belly churned as I felt myself collapsing even more. I did not want to be feeling this, but I was. These feelings surprised and scared me. It wasn't the first time I didn't want to be on this earth.

My thoughts pivoted. What would it be like to jump out of the hotel window and land on the hard pavement below ~ to end it all? It would be so easy to step onto my 8th floor balcony... and jump. It might hurt to hit the pavement, but it would be over quickly. The thought felt enticingly relieving, yet I also felt fear. Was I really ready to let go of everything? I wasn't sure.

A voice inside said, *"Let's think about it and sleep on it ~ doing something impulsively is not always a good idea."* My mind raced back and forth.

"Ok, slow down," I finally said to myself, *"you are exhausted. Just go to sleep now. Maybe you'll feel differently in the morning."* I dragged myself into bed.

That night, I had a powerful, life-altering dream. In the dream, I jumped. I jumped off the balcony and found myself in free fall. It was scary. It was freeing. I had no idea what was going to happen. I was falling. Then suddenly, I landed safely in a soft bed of beautiful pink, orange, and red Chrysanthemums. On one side of me was my beloved tabby cat, Pumpkin. On my other side was a sweet, white dog. In the dream I felt surprised... shocked actually. Those feelings were mixed in with relief and a little bit of delight at landing in this sweet nest of color, aliveness and love. This dream would be a life-changing and life-affirming blessing, truly a gift of support from the Universe.

I woke up from the dream and something had shifted. I felt different, curious, and slightly relieved. I hadn't journaled in years, but I knew I must write. I pulled out my pen. With colorful markers, I drew the orange and pink flower bed, and myself with a little smile, surrounded by animal love. I decided then and there to start listening to my inner world, which I had been neglecting for years. I decided to choose ME.

This dream was a gift so precious, so loving, it would radically re-orient me. For the first time, I felt the possibility that something bigger was holding me. My creative subconscious gave me the beautiful gift of jumping off the balcony and landing in a new experience. I was held, loved and nourished. Something was shifting inside. I felt a seed of strength, clarity and inner knowing. I knew I needed to participate in the next steps of my life. I needed more support to take self-loving action to create the next chapter.

I began to listen to myself and make decisions based on what seemed right for ME. This was hard at first. I was used to focusing on others' needs and ignoring my own. I took one small step at a time, courageously asserting myself. And with every tiny step, I stood in my value, even with discomfort, and the next time, speaking up for my needs ~ for myself ~ became a little easier.

I decided to work with a creativity coach, and I also studied Intentional Creativity painting with Shiloh Sophia McCloud. I hadn't painted in 20 years, but I had always wanted to be in the company of women reconnecting with their creativity in an empowered way. Whatever was holding me back, I knew I was going to work through it with this group of women, because I couldn't do it alone. That support buoyed me while I was in the hotel for the next four months. Even though every day was challenging, I told myself lovingly and firmly: *"You are going to continue to paint even though you're in this hotel room. This time you are not going to collapse."*

I remember buying my first 2 ½ foot by 3 ½ foot canvas. I needed to transport it from my car into the hotel room, but it was almost as tall as my five-foot frame. As I awkwardly carried it into the hotel lobby and tried to put it on a luggage cart, I cautiously looked around, hoping that the staff wouldn't start asking questions.

I got it up to the 8th floor, set up an art space in my room with plastic sheeting taped to the walls, and I painted. Wow, did I paint! It felt so good. The very first words of intention I boldly painted on the blank canvas were: *"I claim my right to exist on this planet and to have the life that I came here for!"* I had never stated anything so boldly before.

When my teacher instructed us to paint the hidden parts of us, to express the layers of shame and rage, I felt nervous at first.

Her words were an invitation: "Choose whatever colors you feel drawn to."

I chose reds, blacks, and deep purples and then let the paintbrush go to town. I put the canvas on the hotel room floor, and with wild abandon, I let the colors fly. I let the tears flow, mixing in with the paint. I pounded the canvas with my big paintbrush. I didn't care how it looked. I cared how it felt ~ which was amazingly free and powerful.

Fifty years of pent-up life-force energy, finally erupting like a volcano of power and color.

I was being fed and nourished by my creative process, which was literally saving my life. The painting that emerged was about reclaiming myself, my energy, and my rhythm. Not the rhythm of a dutiful daughter. Not the rhythm of a pressured over achiever. *My* rhythm.

Slowly, through the layers, She emerged. A powerful Divine Feminine face, full of wisdom, presence, power and vision. I called her "She is My Rhythm." Through the paintbrush, I poured out my pain, grief and outdated patterns, and there She was. She gazed at me, seeing ME, her eyes and expression a reflection of my true Self.

Since I made that bold commitment to myself, more amazing things started to open up. I quit my stressful mental health clinic job and sold my condo. I decided to listen to my heart's desire to get out of the city into a quieter, greener area. When I arrived at the open house for the sweet country cottage rental in Sebastopol, my heart dropped when I saw over 20 people in line to apply. Even though I felt despair, I decided to stay in line ~ I didn't give in.

The landlord skeptically stared at me over her COVID mask, "Why do you want to move here from Oakland?"

Doubt crept in. I began to wonder why I was even trying to get this cottage. Then a strong, loving voice inside of me said, *"No, I get to want this. It's perfect for me. It has everything I want and need. I get to imagine myself in a place like this."* I wanted it so badly, the next day I made the almost three-hour drive, tax return in hand, and a letter explaining why I was the right tenant.

Three days later, I got a call from the landlord. She offered me the cottage.

I was overwhelmed with excitement and disbelief. It took a while to sink in. Could I feel this much joy? Could I imagine moving into a home space where I could create my art and feel safe and nurtured in a beautiful location, surrounded by nature? Could I feel worthy of having something I really truly wanted?

My Soul answered: *"Yes. I could."*

My creative consciousness, my Soul's inner knowing, had guided me, and I finally started to listen ~ really listen ~ to the quiet knowing within. Life had brought me to my knees, and I questioned going on living. In that surrender, something sacred emerged. My creative spirit, that I had been depriving and was buried beneath outdated beliefs, revealed itself as a life-saving force. I began to trust myself and recognize that my needs mattered, that my Soul's desires were valid, and that something larger was guiding me. It took courage to turn inward, to choose myself, and to believe I could live a life shaped by truth and inner calling.

My creative spirit became a steady companion, a compass, a safe place to return to. My creativity now assists me to stay grounded and honest, even when I don't know what's ahead. My divine creative spirit reminds me: *"I am enough, I have value, and I'm free to live fully as myself."*

In my country cottage, I live with a sense of vitality and possibility each day. I wake to birdsong and Camellia blossoms, and fall asleep hearing the owls under a sky full of stars. I feel the joy of connection to both the world and my inner Divine Self. I'm creating art and showing my work in my own gallery space, while walking forward with trust in my own rhythm. I'm opening to romantic love again, this time grounded in self-worth and clarity. Through in-person and online workshops, I'm teaching women how to paint, and express themselves from their Soul's spark, wildness, and inner knowing.

My creativity holds all of me: my sorrow, my fire, my wisdom, my joy. My creative spirit reminds me that I am whole. This journey has been a return, a reclamation, a divine unfolding into the fullness of who I am. I'm deeply grateful for the life-saving dream that began it all ~ a leap off the ledge into the unknown, and a soft landing in that colorful nest. The flowerbed of support and love became the symbol of my transformation. I know now, when I trust myself and the divine, I come home to my Self, and who I really am.

About Aimee Tomczak, MA, LMFT

Aimee Tomczak, MA, LMFT is a psychotherapist, artist and Intentional Creativity painting instructor. With a background in dance, performance, meditation and visual arts, she views creative expression as a transformative practice for self-discovery. Her artwork can be seen virtually and in person at Fulton Crossing Gallery.

In her popular "Awaken Your Creative Portal" workshops, she guides people to reclaim their creative spark and inner wisdom through the Art as Medicine process. She also offers private sessions using creativity for transformation and healing, online and in person. Aimee brings a heartfelt presence, playful compassion, and depth to her teaching and has been called a "Creative Catalyst" by many.

Workshops and More: www.aimeetomczak.com

Artwork: www.aimeetomczakart.com

Contact: Beloved3me3@gmail.com

Free Gift: "Claim Your Creative Space Meditation"
https://mailchi.mp/7b5c0f82c0c9/ylgfnz1ybp
or Scan QR code below.

Chapter 13

RECLAIMING SACRED RADIANCE:
A HEALER'S JOURNEY FROM BURNOUT TO BLESSING

Maureen P. Murphy, DC

When a medical intuitive told me that my seventh chakra was completely closed, as if I had shut a trap door at my crown preventing me from receiving Universal guidance and energy, I was intrigued.

Then she asked, "What percent of you still wants to be on the planet?"

Now I was shocked. I hedged and said, "Sixty percent?"

"Oh no!" she pushed back, "Not for your family, but for YOU."

Wow! How had she intuited this secret I had barely let myself know? I sheepishly admitted it was more like *twenty percent*. Even as I uttered those dangerous words, I felt strangely relieved. It was perplexing yet simple, and true. At that moment, I did not feel the need to argue, defend, justify, or even understand. I simply wanted to know what to do next. She told me my priority was to "pray gratitude" hourly. So, I did.

This is a story about burnout. About a physical breakdown at the threshold of midlife that led to a spiritual awakening and creative upwelling. It's about choice: how my illness offered me a chance to change course and take full responsibility for my life experiences in a way I had never fully mustered nor mastered before. I learned to ask for help, to nurture my connection with Soul and Spirit as a vital part of my well-being, and so much more!

At the time of my crisis, I had been in a prolonged phase of high output and productivity in my life and career. When I say prolonged, I mean about twelve years. At age twenty-five, I had moved across the country from New York to California to complete a four-year chiropractic degree. This required constant testing, which felt like performing, to graduate at the top of my class, become a licensed professional, and build my private practice in Oakland, CA. Stress was a given. I coped by bullying myself into action with urgency and criticism. Thus began my unwitting habit of abusing adrenaline.

On the cusp of starting my practice, I suffered an unexpected blow to my heart: the breakup of my long-term love relationship and the life-dream of starting a family that seemed to go with it. At thirty-one, I was devastated and had trouble accepting this new version of my future. How could I extend myself to help others when I felt so low? With everything else going on in my life, I simply did not have the emotional tools to process it. Instead, I pushed it out of my mind and hid my broken heart.

I felt so vulnerable and alone. Having left my family and a supportive community behind, I thought I had to figure it all out on my own. As a new graduate, I had a *ton* of student loan debt and suddenly felt intense pressure just to survive. I threw myself into helping my patients and building a successful business. I didn't want to feel my grief, overwhelm and distress, so I drowned it out with action.

Still, I wanted to use my energy more effectively in my work, and reasoned that learning a martial art might help me. Drawn by the mysterious and primal sound of drumming in Golden Gate Park one Sunday, I discovered a Japanese Taiko performing group. Taiko, a dynamic and exciting form of percussion and choreography, captured me immediately. When I saw the young Japanese girls beating their hearts out on the drums with such poise and confidence, I knew I had to join them.

The athleticism Taiko required became a way to channel my unexpressed emotion. I dove full force into my new passion, while keeping my dearest friends at bay with busy-ness. My motto: *Eat, Sleep, Taiko!* Perfect for keeping me flooded with my drug of choice: *adrenaline* ~ until I used it all up.

The reward of accomplishment and the fun of making music together was thrilling. I had stumbled on my soul's desire to co-create. Our dojo (school) produced international events and performed on stages around the country. Training was rigorous; our Sensei used old-school training methods like humiliation to break down the ego. However, the hypermasculine and hierarchical system of our dojo eventually proved unsustainable to me.

I began to have serious physical symptoms. I felt bone-tired all the time. I would fall into bed exhausted, then wake up at 3 AM, alarmed, unable to fall back asleep. My thoughts were jumbled and I had difficulty concentrating at work. My digestion was upset and erratic, and every day I found a shocking amount of hair in my hairbrush. I also experienced a painful episode of shingles ~ right in the middle of Cherry Blossom Festival, which demanded my presence in multiple Taiko performances. Perhaps most frightening to me as a chiropractor skilled in palpation, I could feel swollen lymph glands in my groin. My first thought was cancer.

It might surprise you that even with these symptoms, I didn't seek help right away, especially as a healer who knew that these symptoms were serious. Why had I not seen this coming? Clearly I was in denial! I had ignored my pain and the causes of my deepest unhappiness, as well as the choices that could have led to different outcomes. My default: *Don't just sit there, do something!*

I've since learned the term "protective cognition," which accurately describes my habit of dissociating from overwhelming feelings and circumstances I believed I could not change. Besides, I had convinced myself I was doing all the right things. I was exercising daily and eating an impeccable diet. I was making a living doing work I loved, and as my own boss, I could set my own schedule. My practice had grown to include a satellite office in San Francisco, where I lived. I drove a new car, and I was even dating again. On the outside it looked like I had everything together. But on the inside....

When I finally paused long enough to ask myself **why** I was not seeking help, I discovered I was terrified of receiving a terminal diagnosis. More than that, I realized I did not have the will to fight for my own life. **This was my wake-up call ~ a humble reckoning!**

THE POWER OF CHOICE

I decided to break through my fear and denial by confiding in a trusted friend and colleague. Later, a nurse practitioner followed up with blood and stool tests. I was diagnosed with malnutrition. (What?!) Despite my healthy habits, I had been nourishing my ego, not my soul. Additionally: low cortisol, low estrogen, and low progesterone. The diagnosis: adrenal fatigue, early onset perimenopause, parasitic infection. She prescribed a variety of supplements, herbs and REST.

CHOICE TO PRIORITIZE MY WELL-BEING

I knew I had to make radical changes to my life and how I spent my energy. As emotionally painful as it was, it was time to quit the Taiko dojo. Ironically, I had just been placed in the starting lineup of the performance group, a long-cherished goal which signified that Sensei trusted me. I was ready and good enough. I gave up my responsibilities there, and said goodbye to my shocked bandmates. I drove home, sobbing all the way.

Making the decision to preserve my health, even if it meant letting others down, was met with huge support from the Universe. The very next day I received a compelling invitation. Former Taiko Dojo members whom I had always looked up to as my *senpai* (a term of respect given to more experienced students) asked me to join them in a collaborative dance project at *San Francisco Dance Mission Theater*.

I couldn't believe it! My sacrifices at the dojo had paid off. I now had the chance to collaborate with high caliber performers. We co-founded *Taiko Ren*, a non-hierarchical, leaderless performing group. It was a joyful and highly creative reunion. We built our own drums, composed our own songs, and performed locally.

Unfortunately, my body really needed a *complete* rest. Within two years, I let go of my role in *Taiko Ren* too. I surrendered ~ peacefully this time, and began re-evaluating my life and choices.

CHOICE TO REFLECT AND FEEL

In the still-time that followed, it became obvious that much of my pain was the result of avoiding feelings. Projecting a perfect image of myself to mask the persistent unloving thoughts in my head was costly. Criticism, judgment, blame, and guilt had the effect of poisoning me, convincing me I was defective, unworthy, and unlovable.

At the time of my burnout, I was living in a very comfortable San Francisco apartment with lots of light and stunning views. Because I lived alone, I let myself speak aloud the stream of thoughts running through my mind, most of them brutal and negative. I soon recognized their toxicity. What else could be going on inside?

I continued my self-exploration, reasoning that it would be good to bring these thoughts to light. I even caught myself walking down the street saying vile things out loud such as, "*You piece of shit, you lazy ass!*" or other attacks on my being. So, I decided to face myself and vocalize these words while looking in the mirror. I found that when I looked at myself sincerely, I could not continue this diatribe for long. I had glimpsed my innocence and vulnerability, the goodness in my soul. I could no longer insult myself this way.

It was a powerful experiment, but I don't recommend it be done casually. Steeping in the toxic stew of verbal negativity can be too harsh on your cells. Self-examination requires preparation and fortitude. To know difficult things about yourself, you have to develop spiritual and psychological fitness.

CHOICE TO CONNECT, LEARN AND GROW

I began the transition to a new phase of my life. I moved back to Berkeley where I had more friends and my commute would be less stressful. I began to spend my time walking the Berkeley Hills, cooking fresh organic veggies from the farmers market, and listening to inspiring teachers on the radio or CD. I even started studying Spanish. I hosted parties in my home and reconnected with old friends.

My resourceful colleague recommended I consult Christel Nani, a medical intuitive near San Diego. Even though it felt risky to invest in myself, I sought her guidance. I flew to San Diego, rented a car and stayed in a hotel by myself. It was Christel who surprised me by asking how much I still wanted to be alive. And

Christel who suggested I "pray gratitude" every day. Admittedly, there were days when all I could feel thankful for was, "*It's not raining in my bed.*" Nevertheless, the practice of turning my attention towards what was working in my life, instead of what wasn't, shifted my energy and receptivity.

Likewise, my energy brightened when I attended Kirtan events. Kirtan, the call and response practice of chanting the names of the Divine in Sanskrit, welcomes all voices. I quickly felt its benefits. I would come in like a dirty sponge and leave like a clean sudsy one! I gifted myself with a trip to Guatemala for a ten-day Kirtan/Yoga retreat. This practice greatly helped me sense and nurture the Divine within me.

I let my intuition draw me to various teachings. I studied the coach approach and learned several coaching modalities. A new world opened up for me as a student, teacher, and healer. From teachers Morty and Shelley Lefkoe, I learned a powerful process to break through my limiting beliefs and free myself of reactivity and limitation. It forms the core of my coaching with clients today. Another friend introduced me to Julia Cameron's *The Artist's Way* and we studied it together. Here I developed the discipline of writing daily morning pages, which I continue to this day. I joined Lee Glickstein's *Speaking Circles*, a practice group for developing presence when speaking to groups. Allowing myself to be fully seen and heard by others ~ without performing ~ was a life changing skill for me!

Therapy helped me when my mom had a sudden depressive-psychotic episode that took us by surprise. I needed help adjusting to the fact of mental illness in my family. "*Could it happen to me? What was my new role to be?*" I started going to 12-step meetings and learned how to feel safe in groups. I came out of isolation and learned to keep the focus on myself.

Maureen P. Murphy

CHOICE TO DO THE INNER WORK

When I first came out of denial, I grappled with overwhelming shame. I was a doctor who had failed to protect her own health and I felt like a fraud. I wanted to know: what made me vulnerable to burnout? I discovered that empathy, when not acknowledged or developed, could be a two-edged sword. This inquiry gave me the insight to create *The Seven Essential Resilience Skills*, a curriculum and assessment to help other professionals prevent burnout and truly flourish.

A foundational cause of my burnout was spiritual neglect. I believed I had been walking my talk yet had overlooked a key component: nurturing my connection with Source. Even though I thought of myself as a spiritual person, I had been taking my spirituality for granted, phoning it in and forgetting about it. By keeping busy so the bad feelings couldn't find me, I inadvertently stopped feeding the Holy within me. Gradually I became disconnected from Soul and Spirit. As I healed, I came to appreciate that Spirit is ever-evolving. I need to keep up, so I continue on my path of conscious evolution.

The well of sadness was deep. I had fooled only myself, and let myself down. A flood of heavy emotions followed, but this time I felt them fully. Fear, shame, grief, sadness, resentment, anger, and jealousy ~ I felt them all. Then emerged self-hatred, and self-loathing. And finally, remorse that I had never let myself feel joy.

I felt broken beyond repair. A familiar rhyme started playing in my head, "*All the King's horses and all the King's men couldn't put Humpty Dumpty together again.*" As I stood in the shower one morning, the hot water and steam softening my defenses, a new thought slipped in. **Humpty Dumpty was an egg!** He was always meant to crack open ~ to evolve into something more. I realized I was not alone in this very human experience. My crisis was an opportunity to become someone more.

Making the decision to seek help put me on the path of healing. It helped to share my story with trusted friends and colleagues, and to strengthen new relationships more aligned with who I was becoming. I sought out different perspectives and new experiences. I travelled, attended workshops, practiced Yoga and meditation, and found inspiration in nature.

The fruits of these practices were honesty, freedom, reliable connection, and self-love. Mindful awareness allowed the deeper, truer, more essential parts of me to surface and be integrated. I developed real alternatives to the fear, dissatisfaction, and blame I usually projected outward.

AWAKENING IN LOVE

I believe the root of our human suffering stems from the mistaken idea that we are separate from one another and the creative life force. My work with clients centers on recognizing this misunderstanding and turning towards one another with compassion.

As I turned towards myself with compassion and love, a true renaissance followed. I was in bliss! There were days when I could not wait to get home after work so I could spend time letting Love flow in and through me. The early onset of winter nights propelled me to burrow under my soft flannel comforter and let myself feel the love, crying with a sense of relief and joy. I was falling in love with my *real* self. I was so happy to have come home to her. I belonged! I was not separate after all. I remembered these lines from the poem, *Desiderata*, which we sang in 3rd grade choir. I was brought back to the Spring Concert, standing on the risers in the gymnasium, singing, *"...you are a child of the Universe, no less than the trees and the stars, you have a right to be here..."*

It felt like a state of Grace! When I shared this insight with a therapist, she remarked how wonderful it was that I came to this perspective on my own, that I would not confuse it with some dogma or guru outside of myself. That comment stuck with me.

CREATIVE UPWELLING

At first, I had trouble finding words to describe the enormity of what I was experiencing. Phrases like *"Love is all there is!"* and *"I've been born again!"* felt limiting. Then I started receiving downloads of poetry and song. Waking up gifted with words, I would rush to my journal to commune with my muse, sip my tea and bask in the morning light. It felt incredible to be inspired this way! I entertained myself for hours walking the San Francisco Bay trails, re-working and reciting poems to myself. Some came with original tunes playing in my head, even though I am not a musician or singer. I asked my friend Jane DeCuir, a gifted singer-songwriter, what I should do with these songs. She told me to sing them to myself, that they were my medicine.

One afternoon coming back from lunch, I was softly singing a song about finding my way to love, when I noticed the meter-man giving out parking tickets. It was a sunny day and I remember deliberately choosing not to give away my good mood. I could easily have gone down the rabbit hole of resentment and despair. Instead, I thought, *"Well, I can hardly wait to see the good that comes of this. Maybe Oakland needs this money more than I do."*

I spontaneously rolled down my window as he walked by and said in a cheerful voice, *"You wouldn't want to take this back now, would you?"*

He surprised me by smiling and saying, *"Sure! No one has ever asked me so nicely."* WOW! I burst into tears because it was such a powerful and quick response to my internal shift in perspective.

Yes, I was grateful! My radiance was restored and I felt the good flowing in my life. I was invited to share my poems and songs at artists' salons and even had them published in magazines. I moved to a new home, a beautiful cottage with a garden. I bought new clothes, let my hair grow long and experimented with a more feminine expression in my appearance and way of being. As I relaxed and felt less defensive, I enjoyed more freedom in sexual relationships, had more fun, and felt more satisfaction. I no longer needed to control everything and opened to receiving help from friends and unseen allies.

My natural curiosity about my inner workings led me on an illuminated path of healing. Acceptance came more easily and I didn't judge myself for having such strong negativity. I came to recognize how vital my spiritual and mental fitness practices are to my overall health and well-being.

YOUR POWER TO CHOOSE ~ AN INVITATION

Connection in community was crucial to my healing. And that's what I share now ~ especially with women. We humans are wired for connection. When our connections feel threatened, our nervous system reacts with survival mode. We survived and flourished by activating the feminine qualities of cooperation and sharing.

In my role as a resilience and mindset coach, I teach women how to connect to themselves, to others and to the animating spirit of life. I have seen what happens when we lose connection with our Soul and fall out of alignment with our true path. The need to belong is powerful, primal. Realizing we are already connected is the quest of our time.

So how can we cultivate awareness of our belonging and nurture our divinity?

Remember the women you met in this book. Take courage from our stories. My hope is that they inspire you to explore and strengthen your own connection with the Divine. We are witnessing a time of renewal for women, the Divine Feminine rising again in our consciousness. Through technology, we are finding each other and creating opportunities to heal and grow. Still, change comes from practice, not gathering more information. Your invitation is to choose practices every day that encourage your awareness and presence, so you can better sense your true belonging ~ even through the dark times.

ABOUT MAUREEN MURPHY, DC

Maureen Murphy, DC guides extraordinary women who are facing creative blocks, challenging life transitions, or emotional triggers in key relationships, to instead connect wholeheartedly with their guiding passion and purpose, restore their inner radiance, and confidently express themselves at home and at work.

With over three decades experience as a holistic chiropractor, resilience coach, and mindfulness trainer, Maureen has seen firsthand how misalignment with your true self robs you of vitality. Her laser focused methods help you get unstuck and into flow, so you can stop being mad at yourself and start feeling the joy and satisfaction of your success.

Maureen lives with her beloved partner in the heart of Mexico, where she delights in writing poetry, learning salsa dancing, and leading retreats.

MY GIFT TO YOU: *The Emotional Artistry E-Book* ~ Learn to harness vital emotions so you can inspire flow in your creative process, harmony in relationships, and resilience when facing challenges.

https://www.maydayresilience.com/gift-from-maureen *or* Scan QR code below.

Chapter 14

FROM TEARS TO TREASURE

Catherine Smith Bass, EA

"Very truly I tell you, you will weep and mourn while the world rejoices. You will grieve, but your grief will turn to joy."

~ John 16:20 ~

It was March 30th, 2019, right in the heart of tax season. The phone rang around 7:30 PM. When I answered, there was silence on the other end, though I could see that it was my brother-in-law. I could tell something was very wrong.

Concerned, I said, "Are you there? What's wrong?"

He finally conjured up the courage to say the words, "Jason is gone."

I immediately knew what he meant. I could feel it in my bones. He said that my husband had drowned, but he didn't have any details about what had happened. We both cried. Then he said he was coming over so he could be with me while I told my children. My son was twelve, and my daughter was fifteen. Telling them was, by far, the hardest thing I have ever had to do.

We would have been married for 25 years had he made it to September. Jason was only 46 years old, and it felt like he had so many more years of life ahead of him. He was strong and in good shape. It just didn't make sense that he drowned. It was a nice sunny day, so he overestimated the temperature of the water which was around 42°F. He swam about 50 yards out to retrieve his kayak, but went under right before he got there.

From that day forward, my entire life was turned upside down, sideways, and every which way. With it happening during the busiest time of year for me as a tax preparer, my stress level was already high, and this increased my anxiety immensely. But I survived, and I learned so many life lessons along the way.

As I started writing this chapter, I realized how much healing and grieving I still had to do. All I could think of were my traumas, both as a child and as an adult, rather than my money story which was what I originally intended to write about. But I soon realized it was all connected, and that I had to make changes within myself. I had to go through the weeds to get to where I was going. So, I allowed myself to just write, and write, and write until I got to the heart of my issues.

It has been five years since that horrendous day. The fog is lifting, and I want to live again. *"But who am I? What am I here for? What do I want out of my life?"* Now, at age 53, I'm finally figuring out who I am and what my purpose in life is.

REALIZING MY WORTH

I used to believe my husband and I were a team, and that my hopes and dreams for the future were tied to us being together. He was the protector, and I was the caregiver. Now I had to learn to be both, and make all the decisions by myself.

When it came to my marriage, I could honestly say, "I love my husband unconditionally." Jason, however, did not understand what unconditional love was. As much as he wanted to comprehend it, and he attempted to many times during our marriage, he just didn't get it.

My husband was very good at hiding the fact that he never saw himself as worth anything. He portrayed a very confident demeanor. He was known as "Professor Jason" at his job because he could make a tool out of anything, and he could solve any problem that arose. He worked in construction, especially excelling in drywall. But he was also a "jack-of-all-trades" and had his own business where he did various jobs, including setting up stages for football games and concerts. He was also known as "Spiderman," a nickname earned when he built casinos, worked on high rise jobs, and crawled around in the rafters at the local stadium.

He took his superhero status seriously. Right after we first met, he saved a woman's child that was stuck in her car after she had crashed into a semi-truck and her car was pinned under the trailer. The mom was running around screaming for help, and Jason just happened to be in the right place at the right time. So, naturally, he jumped in to help. That was his instinct ~ he acted without even thinking about the consequences.

Not only was he physically strong, but he was also very strong-willed. If he made up his mind to do something, he would accomplish it. I often looked up to him for this ability. One example of this was when our daughter was born, he quit smoking. He succeeded in breaking a twenty-year habit. He made it look easy. He made the decision, smoked his last cigarette, and that was it. Regrettably, he picked it back up after ten years when his father passed away, and he didn't know how else to handle his grief.

Unfortunately, he had been dealt a bad hand when he was born. I always knew that he had no control over his childhood, so I tried to love him through his issues and thought I could "fix" him. Boy, was I wrong. He had to want to fix himself. I couldn't do it for him. But his issues were deep—so deep, in fact, that he only acknowledged his traumatic history of sexual abuse in the year before he died. I can only imagine the shame and guilt he felt over all those years.

Jason did not think he deserved peace. He also believed there was no God... why would He let that happen to a child? This led to his drug abuse and narcissistic ways. But I was in denial about it for our entire marriage. I chose to live by my heart instead of by my head. It's funny how you don't see gaslighting when you're in it, but it becomes crystal clear when you get out of it. He isolated me from my friends and family, picked petty arguments all the time, and manipulated me when he didn't get his way.

As much as my husband had egotistical tendencies, he wanted to be a good person. He just struggled to keep that person at the forefront. At his core he wanted to love 100%, but he just had never been shown how. He was hurt as a child and didn't know how to pick up the broken pieces, so his fears took over.

I tried my best to help him. I had made a commitment, and I was going to see it through. In my mind, he was a victim of circumstance. It wasn't his fault. *"How could I abandon him?"*

Still, I wondered, *"What is wrong with me? Why do I keep searching for love in all the wrong places? Am I worthy of love?"*

Well, the answer is yes. I *am* worthy of love and so much more. I feel like I am awakening to a new world, or at least a world that I can see more clearly.

I had to sit down and do some deep introspection. *"Why did I put up with that? How can I fix it now?"*

During my grief and confusion, part of me thought: *"Am I as broken as my husband was?"*

The more I thought about it, the answer was *"No, I'm not."*

I realized it was his destiny to die young, not mine, and I had been carrying his burdens. I had to look in the mirror and figure out why. Once I started asking the questions, I started getting the answers. I now know that I am worthy of self-love, and I deserve to live in abundance.

After his death, I realized that I hadn't been able to help him heal from his wounds like I wanted to. I believed that his narcissistic behavior was normal. I had been raised by a narcissist. I didn't know any better. This is why I had to learn to love myself again and prioritize my own well-being. As a mother and caretaker, it's hard to put yourself first. But self-love is so important to our ability to care for others. And most of all, I had to forgive myself for loving people who were broken.

Forgiveness became one of the most powerful tools I had. I realized that my heart carried the weight of grief and other people's actions until I forgave them. I learned that it is not about forgetting the wrongs; it's about refusing to let them control your life. True strength is not holding on. True strength is letting go. We can use our most painful experiences to bring healing to others.

THE LESSONS FROM MY GRIEF

The moment I became a widow, I was terrified that I would become so consumed with grief that I wouldn't be able to pick myself back up again. I had two children who relied on me, and suddenly I was the only parent they had left. *"How dare I take the time to grieve? Who has time for that?"* I had to support my kids emotionally and financially, and I had a business to run.

I had also just lost my boss and mentor eight months prior to my husband's death. He was like a father to me. But again, I didn't have time to grieve. There was always something more important to do. So, I kept shoving it back inside, telling myself *"I'll deal with it later ~ when I have time."*

Clients began passing away. I attended funeral after funeral, which put a huge toll on my heart. I naturally became a support for other widows during this time. I became a safe person with whom they could talk about what they were feeling, emotionally and financially. I've been there.

When I was in ninth grade, my nephews (ages six, five, and six months) died when their home burned to the ground. I had never cried so much. I became deeply depressed and didn't want to live anymore. My mom got frustrated, sat me down, and told me I had to snap out of it. "Life doesn't stop when someone dies," she told me. "You must go on." So that's exactly what I did. I just kept going through the motions of life until enough time had passed that I felt "normal" again. Thankfully, when I went back to school, my friends were there to support me; they helped me find my will to live again.

I realized that this early trauma of losing my nephews when I was thirteen was similar to the loss of my husband. In other words, I reacted the same way. I had the same fears, and my perspective hadn't changed with age. Now, I realized I needed to grieve for them all. So, I gave myself the space to feel and process the grief instead of running away from it. I found safe places and moments to reflect and grieve.

After I became a widow, I read book after book until I felt like I understood grief. Or I at least realized that everyone goes through all stages of grief, but everyone's path to healing is different. We all grieve in our own way, and our brain processes grief based on our memories and belief systems. But essentially, we never actually "get over it." It just gets a little easier with time.

Grief is love that never dies!

HEALING MY BODY, MIND, AND SPIRIT

Now, I am prioritizing my physical health and developing healthier habits. I have started working with a holistic medical practitioner to address my thyroid issues, specifically hyperthyroidism. My entire diet and eating habits have changed. I even learned to stop eating sugar, and started drinking water instead of sweet tea. And I became more active. All these changes calmed and grounded my body, helping me feel more balanced.

Next, I healed from the narcissism that I had dealt with for my entire life, from my mother to my husband. I learned to see my own value instead of seeing it through the eyes of someone else. I changed my mindset and healed from these limiting beliefs.

For example, after my mom's funeral, Jason started a fight with me. He could not have picked a worse day. How selfish of him to insert his needs over mine. Looking back, he just didn't know how to help me process my grief. He disliked seeing me sad, and wanted to help. But all he knew how to do was distract me with an argument.

My mother was also a narcissist, which I didn't realize until recently. That has been very eye-opening as well. When I was a child, I put her on a pedestal and admired her so much—she could do no wrong. She was a strong woman who could accomplish anything she put her mind to. I wanted to be just like her. In hindsight, I was always looking for her approval and just wanted to be loved and accepted by her. I was searching for something I could never receive.

One memory I have of my mother is a little disturbing. We lived down the street from a Baptist church. Throughout my childhood, I had to walk to and from church every Sunday by myself while she slept in. She felt that because she had already gone to church as a child, there was no need to go as an adult. I had realized that she was being a hypocrite. Eventually, my friends and I would hang out at the park down the street while our parents thought we were in church. My mom found out shortly after that, and soon I quit going altogether. But I still appreciate the foundation I received, because I remember a lot of the Bible now that my relationship with God has been healed.

RECONNECTION WITH GOD

This process of grieving, healing, and rebuilding myself laid the foundation for a new relationship with God. The energy I call God is another new presence in my life. He has always been there, but I pushed Him aside while being raised by a mother and married to a husband who did not believe. Even though I miss them both dearly, I believe they have made their way home to God and are finally at peace—something they could not find here on earth.

After losing my nephews, I did not understand how God could take three innocent children. I had become very distant from Him, and it took me forty years to make my way back. I embraced many other religions along the way. I always felt connected to the universe or a higher power, but I felt that there was no God. I still don't like the fact that I lost my nephews, but now I feel like He saved them from a life of hardship. Their mother was schizophrenic, and both parents had alcohol issues. Maybe this is how I justify it in my head, but I know that God had a reason. I may not know what it was, and I may never figure it out. But I have made peace with it.

While grieving, I found solace and healing through prayer, meditation, and studying the Bible, which led to a deeper connection with God. I developed strong intuition and learned to trust in divine guidance. I realized that I had to stop blaming God for death. And that I will be with my people again in Heaven one day. My faith is strong and resilient now, and I see God as the light again. I am grateful for what He provides. I feel God and love all around me, sometimes in the most surprising places.

TRANSFORMATION INTO ABUNDANCE

I was tired of living paycheck to paycheck, always scrambling to pay for unexpected expenses. I was ready for the stability of a savings account, and I was ready to stop having to find creative ways to pay the bills. Jason did not believe that he deserved wealth. He always sabotaged himself any time that either one of us made good money. I wanted to save it, while he would always find a way to spend it. He couldn't help himself. To me, it felt like an incurable disease. It was a cycle that continued throughout our entire life together, a cycle I needed to end once and for all.

Our limitations are often tied to our childhood traumas, no matter how big or small they are. I used to think because I wasn't beaten or abused that I didn't have any issues. But that could not have been further from the truth. Everything affects your psyche in some way. Since I changed my mindset, my life has completely transformed.

It is so empowering to be able to say *"No"* to challenging clients. Instead of chasing money, I am making money. I have grown my business, I have my own office space for my practice, and I answer only to myself. I now have win-win relationships with my clients, which is so much better and more rewarding for both of us. And my relationship with money has grown, along with my healing.

Money is great, but... *"What am I really here for?"* It's not just about preparing taxes or helping people out of their IRS problems. Those things are important, but I want to help people resolve their money issues once and for all. I found that my grief has given me a gift that I can use to help other widows overcome the things that are holding them back and build a new life for themselves.

We may feel we are not worthy enough to be wealthy. We think people with money are evil. One of the most popular sayings is: "Money is the root of all evil," which leads us to believe we will change for the worse. But what I have realized is ~ I will still be myself with the money. I will choose to use my abundance for good. It will only change me if I let it.

I used to think wealth came from working harder, putting in more hours, earning bonuses, or winning the lottery. But that's not how it works. Money flows in many ways. And very fast, I might add. You must be grateful for the money coming in, but also for the money going out. Be thankful that you have money to pay your bills, not upset that you have bills to pay. And have gratitude for what those bills provide for you. It's not about the amount of money. It's about the freedom to do what you want.

Once my mind, body, and spirit came into alignment, my entire life changed. Now I live with a higher purpose and with more gratitude than ever. I learned that being thankful for everything—the good, the bad, and the ugly—puts you in a better place to receive the blessings life has to offer.

When I realized I could let go of the things I couldn't control, I became a much happier and more appreciative person. I now know I am worthy of living in abundance. I have more time to enjoy my life and my family. I am no longer desperate for clients. I even have money saved for a rainy day. I bought my first house. I drive a nice SUV. And I am—finally—no longer stressed over finances. I *know* that I deserve wealth and stability. Abundance is a state of mind.

FINAL REFLECTION

The death of my husband shattered my world, but it also became the catalyst that sparked real, lasting change in my life. As painful as it was, it forced me to face the patterns that had kept me stuck for years, and through that uncomfortable work, I found profound healing and transformation.

Through this journey, I discovered my higher purpose: to walk alongside others as they find financial peace and build a mindset of abundance. Today, I have the honor of guiding widows as they heal, grow, and create lives filled with hope and possibility.

There is life, hope, and abundance on the other side of grief.

If my tears can turn to treasure, yours can too!

ABOUT CATHERINE BASS, EA

Catherine Bass, Enrolled Agent, is not just your average tax expert; she is a powerhouse in the world of tax relief and financial empowerment. As the founder of Bass Tax Relief in Arlington, Texas, Catherine has solidified her reputation as a leading authority on resolving individual and small business tax dilemmas with the IRS. With over 25 years of hands-on experience, she has represented thousands of taxpayers.

Beyond her professional credentials. She is a resilient widow, juggling life with two young adult children and two loving dogs. In her downtime, she immerses herself in the joys of reading, hiking, and rocking out at concerts with her daughter.

Now, as she embraces the wisdom of middle age, Catherine has set her sights on helping other women who have faced loss find their way to abundance. Drawing from her own journey through grief, she is passionate about sharing the healing skills she has cultivated. With Catherine, it's not just about taxes, it's about transforming lives.

Email: Cathy@BassTaxRelief.com

Scan the QR code or email Cathy for your Free "Widow's Essential Documents Checklist."

CROSSING BORDERS:
SOUL INITIATIONS
ABROAD

Chapter 15

WELCOME AND GOOD LUCK:
MY IMMERSION AND AWAKENING IN NIGERIA

Debbie Klein, PhD

I savored the plane rides from Tampa to Atlanta to London to Lagos, wishing I could spend more time suspended between worlds. My dreamy state of liminality invited waves of self-reflection and letting go. Upon landing in Lagos, still groggy from sleepless travel, I was thrust into a state of heightened awareness. The madness of the Lagos airport enveloped and then pushed me out into my new reality.

People greeted me enthusiastically, "Ẹ káàbọ̀, òyìnbó!" (Welcome, white person!). Men of all ages tugged at my clothing, asking for money and insisting on carrying my luggage. Somehow, I managed to stave them off as I exited into the dense night air. At long last, my welcoming hosts spotted me in the crowd and whisked me away to the temporary respite of a hostel. The portal to my future had opened, and I was mustering the courage to feel my way through with grace.

I woke up the next day to discover the bustling streets of Lagos, full of unfamiliar sights, sounds, and smells. Lagos overwhelmed my senses. Crowds of women, men, children, armed police, goats, and chickens wove their way through the chaos. Cars, motorcycles, trucks, and vendors competed for their rightful place in the flow. People shouted. Horns honked. Dust clung to my skin as the streets served up a cocktail of diesel fuel, tropical air, and savory stews simmering in palm oil. I drank it all in.

Tunde, a university driver, picked me up at the US embassy and off we went in his faded blue Peugeot 504 to the University of Ibadan or UI for short. Our conversation was sparse, but an eclectic range of jùjú, fújì, and Afrobeat tracks set a festive tone for our four-hour journey. While we hit some traffic jams or go-slows, the roads were in good enough condition for smooth travel.

Once we reached the outskirts of Ibadan, the roads were eroded and difficult to navigate. Tunde got creative, weaving through oncoming traffic to avoid the endless maze of potholes. We finally arrived at the roughly paved road leading up to the UI entrance where armed guards checked the trunk of our car for anything suspicious. Without much fanfare, Tunde deposited me at my new home, Queen Elizabeth Hall, saying, "Welcome and good luck."

I was nineteen, yet I already felt like an old woman in a young woman's body—all too aware of the built-in limits of moving through the world as a woman. I was restless and ready to escape my country's unapologetic values of capital over humanity and ethnocentrism over respect for other cultures. I was grateful for this opportunity of a lifetime to study history, anthropology, and dance in Nigeria. Still, I couldn't help but wonder: what had I gotten myself into?

The University of Ibadan is a beautiful campus with trees and farmland interspersed among its austere cement-block buildings. The campus hummed with the vitality of thousands of students, faculty, and staff. Chickens and goats roamed freely around the living quarters and food canteens.

The campus soundscape was like nothing I had experienced before. At 5 am every morning, my neighbors blasted the latest jùjú album by Shina Peters while a church group sang "J.E.S.U.S" to the tune of the children's "B.I.N.G.O" song. In the mornings and evenings, the campus church filled the air with live gospel interspersed with energetic prayer. The campus mosque called to prayer, "Allahu Akbar, Allahu Akbar, Allahu Akbar," at dawn, noon, late afternoon, sunset, and evening. Throughout the night, shrill calls of small primates sounded like human babies crying, while frog choirs provided a steady backbeat of guttural harmonies.

There were around 17,000 students attending UI, and hundreds more were squatting in dorm rooms with friends. Queens Hall, one of two female-only residential halls, housed over 400 women. Most Queenites squeezed three or more women into their 120-square-foot rooms.

The living conditions were challenging for all of us. Our rooms were indoor/outdoor spaces. My room was on the second floor of the three-story building, right in the middle of the action. A louvered window with uneven slats opened onto the busy corridor, and a back door opened onto a small balcony. There were no screens. A few brightly colored geckos became frequent, and welcome, guests. We enlisted our geckos to help limit the presence of our most unwelcome roommates: the mosquitoes, cockroaches, and rats.

Our balconies became spaces for cooking, washing, drying clothes, and dumping dirty water. Already struggling with my lack of privacy, I avoided lingering on the balcony so as not to draw more attention to myself. When I was out and about, I was always greeted with enthusiastic pointing, jeering, and the white-person song, "Òyìnbó Pepper," referring to the phenomenon of white people turning red while eating hot peppers. There were not many white people at the university or roaming the city of Ibadan on foot, so a rare sighting was noteworthy.

SAVORY STEWS, RAMEN REALITY

I quickly fell in love with Nigerian food. Starches like èbà (cassava flour), àmàlà (yam or cassava flour), rice, and pounded yam were paired with savory tomato-based stews. My favorite stew was èfó (spinach). I also enjoyed the slimy ewedú (okra) and hearty ègúsí (melon seed) stews. The most prized starch, pounded yam, required two or more women to vigorously pound boiled yams with mortars and pestles into a smooth texture. Beef, goat, fish, chicken, eggs, black beans, and fried plantains were tasty additions to any stew. With few exceptions, women prepared the meals.

On campus, women were expected to cook in their rooms. And when they did eat out, it was usually with male companions. As a student with only an electric kettle, I was not equipped to cook in my room. My meals were often limited to oatmeal, ramen, or cornflakes with powdered milk, supplemented with bananas and peanuts. Occasionally, I ate at campus canteens, but my experience was often uncomfortable since these spaces were mostly occupied by men.

NAVIGATING SCARCITY IN SOLIDARITY

In the 1980s, Nigeria's oil-dependent economy collapsed, leading to harsh structural adjustment measures that cut public services. When I arrived in 1990, economic instability and corruption were entrenched. Life became increasingly difficult for anyone relying on government-funded water, electricity, roads, housing, and education.

The city of Ibadan's water infrastructure had not been maintained or updated in decades. Pipes, pumps, and treatment facilities had long since stopped functioning. In our dorm, there was no running water and only intermittent electricity. Every other week or so, tanker trucks delivered water to two giant storage containers in the courtyard behind the dorm.

Whenever there was a delivery, about a hundred of us lined up at five a.m., five-gallon buckets in tow, to gather water from the tanks. We were lucky if any was left by the time we reached the front. Doing our best not to spill a drop, we hauled our buckets up flights of stairs to our rooms. These hard-won buckets had to last until the next delivery, which was never guaranteed. If the water ran out, we shared whatever we had. We used the water for bathing, cooking, and cleaning, careful to save any dirty water for flushing. Bottled drinking water was one of my biggest expenses.

Bathing was a luxury. In both dry and rainy seasons, the air hung heavy with humidity, my body permanently coated in dust and grime. The heat made cold-water baths a shock to the system. We took our bucket baths in an old ceramic tub with no curtains. Soaping up and rinsing with a limited amount of water was neither pleasant nor effective. Washing my thick, shoulder-length hair was nearly impossible, often not worth the effort.

There were not enough bathrooms to accommodate the Queenites. Each floor had just one, with two ceramic, seatless toilets—no doors, no privacy. We flushed manually, using buckets of dirty water we had carefully conserved. Despite our best efforts, the toilets were breeding grounds for maggots and malaria-carrying mosquitoes. I longed for flushing toilets, running water, electricity, and the ability to maintain my personal hygiene.

Still learning how to care for myself in these conditions, I often suffered from stomach discomfort, headaches, and fatigue. Sitting on my thin mattress in front of my desk fan—when the electricity was running—was one of the few ways I found some sweet relief from the daily grind of physical and mental exhaustion. Living in these conditions with my dormmates, in solidarity, is forever etched in my bodily memory. My social and political awareness, along with my capacity for compassion, grew exponentially.

Debbie Klein

CALLING HOME AND LETTING GO

Amidst the struggle to meet my basic needs, maintaining connection with home became its own arduous challenge, testing my patience and resolve. Making phone calls at NITEL (Nigerian Telecommunications Limited) was always an unbearably time-consuming ritual. The journey to make one four-minute call began with a thirty-minute walk in the relentless sun to a bus stop, where I jumped into an already moving VW bus with tightly packed benches of sweaty people. After negotiating with the crowd in my best Yorùbá, I stepped over passengers just in time to jump off at my stop. I walked for another thirty minutes through market stalls and throngs of people, trying not to fall into deep sewage gutters lining the streets, until eventually I arrived at a stark, unpaved open space with a circuitous line of people.

I joined the amorphous queue of customers clamoring for a view of the elusive phone booths that remained hidden behind the sea of patrons until our turn. The rifle-wearing soldiers controlling the crowd always greeted me with expressions of pity. Consuming a whole day and weekly budget, this ritual almost always ended in disappointment. Either calls did not go through to the US, or my family was not home to receive them.

Much to my surprise and delight, a business center with a NITEL office opened just outside the main gate of the UI campus. But, like the one in town, this location was plagued by dysfunction. The communal quest to make calls was still chaotic. Everyone could hear each other's conversations. As time crept by, we all inched closer to the desk shrine displaying the coveted cream-colored landlines with faded buttons. We were not allowed to touch the phones. Dialing the US entailed punching in at least twenty digits, an ordeal that annoyed the employees and usually took three or four attempts to get right.

On the rare occasion when I got through, the crowded room became hauntingly quiet, my curious queue mates hanging on my every word. Just as I began to feel reconnected, the employee monitoring the call abruptly cut the line mid-conversation, as soon as my four minutes were up. This ritual was so disheartening that I had no choice but to let go of my desire to reach home. I was here now.

SUGAR DADDIES AT THE KOKO DOME

When I carved out some time to venture into the town of Ibadan, I enjoyed exploring the Dugbe market and its outskirts—vegetable, fruit, and meat stands, food canteens, hair parlors, cassette vendors, the bookstore, cloth stalls, and more. During one of my excursions, I discovered the Koko Dome, a restaurant located behind the iconic, fire-damaged 25-story building called Cocoa House (West Africa's first skyscraper). Even though I was underdressed, I was able to make it past the armed guards by using my Yorùbá greetings.

Upon entering, I was shocked by the upscale, outdoor ambiance. Tables covered with white cloth circled a giant swimming pool. No one was swimming, but several clusters of European women were sunbathing. The servers were formally dressed. I learned that this was a Lebanese-owned restaurant. They served a range of Lebanese, European, and Nigerian food. I had stumbled upon an exclusive oasis in the middle of the city's chaos.

After indulging in a chicken shawarma wrapped in fresh pita, I was able to notice the clientele. Well-dressed expatriates from Europe and the Middle East, Nigerians, professors, families—it was a scene I would never have expected in the heart of Dugbe. Slowly savoring my Star beer, I noticed many tables of couples. Upon closer examination, I recognized several Queenites from my dorm. They were all dining with much older men.

It took me a moment to register what I was seeing. My dormmates were impeccably dressed in tailored skirts and blouses, matching accessories, and high-heeled shoes. Their hair and makeup were flawless and fashionable. The men wore freshly pressed suits, stylish cuff links, and bright gold watches.

When I returned to the dorm, I was eager to tell my friend, Kehinde, about what I had witnessed at the Koko Dome. Kehinde was one of my best friends. A serious student with an infectious love for life, she was kind and curious about me and my culture. Her style was more like mine, comfortable and understated. We became close friends during my subsequent stays in Nigeria and well after.

Laughing as she imagined this scene through my eyes, she was all too familiar with the sugar daddy culture, as she called it. She told me about the notorious group of older men called sugar daddies who descended upon Queens Hall every weekend to seek potential mistresses or girlfriends whom they would shower with money and gifts. Queens Hall was the hub of a weekly cruising ritual in which men in their Mercedes circled the driveway for hours, taking as much time as needed to scour the parking lot for their dates. This ritual was a spectacle to behold. Campus security was complicit, counting on generous bribes that boosted their meager salaries.

My friends further educated me about the sugar daddy culture by introducing me to Nollywood films, a burgeoning industry at the time. The films dramatized the lives of both men and women involved in these relationships. While the men were often portrayed as self-interested predators, the women were just as often portrayed as clever manipulators who knew how to get what they needed. In the popular film, *The Campus Queen*, Banke uses her beauty, charm, and intelligence to manipulate her sugar daddy, a powerful governor—ultimately exposing corruption in his administration.

SURVIVING MALARIA, A RITE OF PASSAGE

While navigating the social terrain was broadening my worldview and curiosity each day, the physical realities of life in Nigeria began to catch up with me. After one of my classes on the outskirts of campus, I started to feel dizzy, hot, cold, nauseous, achy, and so weak I could barely walk. I kept telling myself I just needed to make it back to my room. But how was I going to walk across campus for thirty minutes in the blistering midday sun when I felt so off balance?

Before setting off on what seemed to be an impossible journey, I needed to find a bathroom. The only one I knew of was in a nearby building, the Institute of African Studies. Unlike the austere functional buildings that defined the campus aesthetic, the Institute stood out—a circular museum-like structure framed by white pillars. Its landscaped grounds featured large cement and metal sculptures of Yorùbá human and spirit figures. An important fixture on the UI campus, the Institute housed a collection of art, a small library, and rooms for lectures and performances.

When I reached the Institute, all I could do was collapse onto the ground, my head on my backpack. Looking up at the sky, I saw the Yorùbá Òrìṣà, Ṣàngó (spirit of thunder, power, and transformation) and Ọṣun (spirit of water, fertility, and beauty) swirling around me. A giant man and woman with large heads and slender bodies were rhythmically swaying in the breeze amidst the trees. Someone tapped me on the shoulder and asked if I was okay. That moment of human connection was sobering, just the right encouragement to get me on my feet. Standing, I checked to see if the sculptures were still animated. Maybe they would follow me home.

I'm not sure how I made it back to my room. I was still delirious, sweating, shivering, and barely able to walk. I hoped I wasn't dying. I lay on my back on the floor, trying to absorb the cement's coolness. Then I reached for my journal and scribbled, desperate to record what I was feeling—and to remind myself I still wanted to live.

I slipped out of consciousness. Having recently read *My Life in the Bush of Ghosts*, I found myself drifting through the dreamlike otherworldliness of Tutuola's forest. That was when my spirit friend first appeared, a yellow-orange bobcat with light brown spots. She glided toward me, placed a paw gently on my shoulder, and vanished into the trees.

My roommate miraculously appeared and enlisted some of our friends to make the journey into town to find Dr. Gupta, a wonderful doctor who treated my friends' recurring cases of malaria. Generously willing to make an after-hours house call, Dr. Gupta found me on the floor of my room.

This was around three months into my stay, and I had come down with my first of many bouts of malaria. I woke up in the guest room of an American couple who worked for USIS, the United States Information Service. Everyone told me I was lucky. I found myself in a large bed in an air-conditioned room. I was freezing. I ate American food and had access to a clean bathroom with running water. Was I dreaming? Was I alive? Was I home? Stunned by how much easier it was to be sick and recover in this environment, I felt eternally grateful for the care and generosity of my friends, Dr. Gupta, and the USIS diplomats. Even in Ibadan, the Americans lived like Americans. Noted.

My memory of those lost days of recovery is fuzzy. Years later, a friend told me that Dr. Gupta had been worried that I might have contracted cerebral malaria. While somewhat rare, malaria of the brain is often deadly. Three months in, I had witnessed most of my friends suffering from bouts of malaria, treating it like the flu. Most Nigerians lived with and survived malaria, except for those who were too young, too old, immune compromised, or unlucky.

Though I struggled to stay healthy, my youthful spirit and old soul kept me going. Surviving malaria became a rite of passage that deepened my humility, strengthened my connections, and marked my initiation into Nigerian life.

UNIVERSITY OF IBADAN ON STRIKE

Before the end of the semester, our faculty went on strike, and classes were cancelled indefinitely. The administration withheld faculty paychecks (again). I learned that even when they were paid, faculty could not live on their salaries. Serving as a professor was a personal sacrifice—a labor of love and a commitment to nurturing future generations.

Soon after the strike was announced, my US university shut down its program in Nigeria. Out of the blue, a professor from my university back home showed up at my dorm room. Dressed in professional clothes, she sat on my rickety desk chair. I was still processing the surreal nature of her visit when she asked how I was doing. Before I could say much, she expressed concern about my health and safety, mentioning she'd heard I had barely survived malaria. How had she even learned about my struggles?

She told me she had called my parents in Florida, warned them I wasn't safe, and urged them to bring me home. But they had refused, trusting me to make the right decision. I hadn't known any of this. Learning that my parents had supported me, I felt overwhelmed with gratitude and relief. Looking a bit confused, the professor stood up to leave, adding that my home university would no longer be responsible for my safety.

I was five months in, and my molecules had already shifted. When basic needs aren't guaranteed, every part of life feels precious.

Back home, the basics were covered, and the drive for personal success seemed to be life's main goal. Here, human connection was everything; we needed each other to survive.

That night, still buzzing from the unexpected visit, I saw my grandmother in a vision. Larger than life, she floated in the sky, dressed in royal purple, the ocean breeze dramatizing her presence. Her warmth comforted and encouraged me. "I'm just getting started," I told her. Deep within, something urged me to stay. Drawing inspiration from my grandmother and the generations of women before me, I felt bolstered by their strength.

Freed from the confines of university life, I was finally able to embark on the journey I had set in motion just before leaving Florida. That weekend, I traveled to meet the family of traditional drummers in Èrìn-Òṣun, who would soon become lifelong friends and collaborators in my doctoral research in anthropology.

ABOUT DEBBIE KLEIN, PHD

Performing with the Àyàn Àgálú troupe in Ilorin, Nigeria (1997)

Debbie Klein is a cultural anthropologist and professor who has taught at Gavilan College in Gilroy, California for over two decades. A dedicated ethnographer, she has spent many years living and working in Nigeria, conducting long-term research with Yorùbá performing artists. During that time, she became proficient in the Yorùbá language and toured southwestern Nigeria as a dancer with a traveling troupe. Her ethnography and articles offer rich insight into the lives, artistry, and perspectives of her collaborators.

Building on this foundation, Debbie's current writing turns inward. Textured with humor and grit, her memoir-in-progress traces her personal transformation as a young woman navigating life in 1990s Nigeria. Through immersive storytelling, she invites readers to move beyond the familiar—to embrace discomfort, trust the unknown, and engage with narratives that deepen empathy and cross-cultural understanding.

Debbie Klein

Now based in California, she draws inspiration from the wildness of the Pacific Ocean, the serenity of the redwood forest, and the majesty of the Sierra Nevada Mountains.

dklein@gavilan.edu
www.debbieklein.org

Chapter 16

FROM VIOLATION TO SOUL INITIATION
IN THE SACRED VALLEY OF PERU

Cheyenne Marie Wright
Astrologer, Soul Tender and Embodiment Midwife

I'll never forget the scratchy, black polyester upholstery, the sparkling night time display that shone from the street lights of Cusco, or the darkness that seemed to stretch on forever as we drove away from the city and into the Sacred Valley...

The dismantling of my reality accelerated... and simultaneously everything seemed to come to a standstill.

I was riding in the front seat of my taxi driver Cristian's 20-year-old Toyota sedan as we neared the road that led through the Peruvian Andes toward the valley.

A burgeoning feeling in my body came to the forefront of my awareness. It became crystal clear that there was a drug inside me, and it was activating. I could barely sense the abrupt shift in my driver's manner through the heavy, drunk feeling that began to permeate my whole body. There was something opportunistic in his shift... He was uncharacteristically giddy, as if looking forward to some delightful surprise I was unaware of...

And then it hit me.

"Why had I left my water bottle in the car when I stepped out for a moment??"

I was witnessing my worst nightmare come to life.

"He wouldn't do that to you. Don't be silly. Don't say anything to him!"

I was shocked by the words bubbling up from the recesses of my own subconscious. Words that diminished the experience that I *knew*, in every cell of my body, was happening. He had put a drug in my water bottle, and now... my body was starting to shut down.

It was going to be an excruciating hour-long night drive at 13,000 ft elevation through dark stretches with no cell service.

But now... I didn't know who the bigger enemy was. The man who had violated my body with a drug that would shut down all my motor functions... or the very programming, alive and well inside my mind, that would sacrifice *my* life in protection of *his*.

It all started seven months earlier, when I was unexpectedly guided to make the Soul-led decision to settle in the Sacred Valley of Peru. After my arrival, I had gotten to know Cristian as a friendly and attentive acquaintance.

That afternoon he was driving me to the nearest city, Cusco, so I could run errands. I needed to go to the bank first, but when we arrived, there was a line that stretched out the door and around the corner. I sighed and queued up. It felt like an unbearably long wait. By the time I got inside the door, I still had to take a number and continue waiting in the line of numbered people before me.

I began feeling incredibly overwhelmed by the atmosphere. I was overcome by the dense, inorganic energy that emanates from the matrix, the banking system—these bureaucratic institutions that feel like they are made to drain the very life-force from you.

I felt immense pressure building, culminating in my head, like I might panic... or explode.

Then, something occurred that I had never experienced before.

I was called inward to enter a deep and profound meditative state. It was like a pendulum swung from the intense density and drainage of life-force energy into that unshakable place of peace and expansiveness within. I was astounded at how deep I went. Having had a spiritual practice for three years, this inner space was familiar, but I had never needed to call upon it in public—and had never been on the verge of a panic attack before.

I felt like I was observing myself throughout the whole experience, from the powerful and surprising amount of frustration and borderline panic to the profoundly deep descent into that spiritual sanctum within. The energy and frequency within me, *and around me*, shifted. Unexpectedly, the line started to move quickly, and soon, I was called to the counter.

I left the bank with a grand curiosity. "*I wonder why all of that just unfolded....*"

It was so remarkable and unusual. I knew it had to have happened for some reason, but as with the language of Spirit, you never know when, or *if*, you will be let in on the secret.

After a day of errands, the back seat was filled with bags, so I was sitting in the front. It was dark outside now, and I needed to make one final stop.

Cristian and I made a plan: I would run into the store, and in fifteen minutes, he'd pull up so I could hop in. In the split second before I got out of the taxi, I grabbed my purse, leaving my water bottle. It would just be a quick run-in, after all.

It all worked out perfectly. I was out in fifteen, and he pulled right up.

He began to make small talk with me again, as we always did. He casually expressed curiosity about the contents of my water bottle. I perked up for the Spanish practice I so enjoyed, since I was a beginner at best. We drove into the busy traffic slowly making our way, about to begin the hour-long drive through the dark mountains and sparse settlements that led back to the first town in the valley, Pisac.

"Es agua pura?" *Is it pure water?*

"¿Cuándo comiste?" *When did you last eat?* "¿Qué comiste?" *What did you eat?*

Upon his mention of my water, I realized how thirsty I was and took a big gulp.

They seemed like innocent questions.

I took in the final sights of the city, the lights twinkling against the backdrop of a dark night.

As we weaved through the chaos of Peruvian traffic, getting closer to the open road that led away from the city, I began to feel a familiar, but shocking feeling. It was an effervescence in my body, like champagne bubbles trickling upwards through my center.

"*Where is this coming from?*" I know this feeling from taking substances like MDMA...

My reality, my trust for this man I had established a relationship with, began to crumble before my eyes.

Realization struck me. In one moment, that felt like an eternity, I *knew* a drug had been put into my water. I realized his questions were *not* innocent; he was gathering intel for a plan. My body turned to lead. I felt I had tripped into a well, slowly falling into the darkness of unconsciousness.

And yet, simultaneously, a shocking narrative began blaring through my mind. "*He wouldn't do that to you. Don't be silly. Don't say anything to him! How embarrassing.* **You** *must be wrong.* **You** *must be mistaken.*"

I was fully overcome by a multidimensional experience—several different parts of me speaking clearly as though they were all on center-stage with spotlights.

There was the tangible, physical part of me mustering every ounce of physical energy to keep my body upright and exude an energy of calm normalcy. With the strenuous effort it took to speak, I responded to his conversation with just enough words to show that nothing was awry, and not a syllable more.

Then there was the desperate voice in my mind, insisting I was ridiculous for thinking he would drug me and that I must be making things up.

And the last part of me, just like earlier in the bank, was looking down at everything unfolding from the observer perspective.

It became obvious I needed to return to that deep inner sanctuary I had accessed earlier, and there, ask my ancestors for the Truth. Shockingly, I entered the inner sanctum with ease. This explained why that ineffable experience in the bank had arisen through me beyond my mental understanding. It was preparation.

As I entered, I felt my great grandmother, "Nana," Frances Reynoso Pinelli, in the guardian angel form she now appeared to me in since I had begun working with her shamanically eight months earlier. I felt her husband, "Da," Victor Pinelli, behind her. There was only one question to ask, quickly and with precision, as I was summoning internal energies with fierce willpower.

Is the worst thing happening?" I asked inside my being.

"*Yes.*"

The answer came so instantaneously, so clear and incisive, it was as though she were in the car with me. My worst nightmare was to be physically compromised and raped, and there, with the precious voice of my great grandmother, was confirmation that it was manifesting.

It was such a striking reality, like an arrow piercing my heart—no time to panic, no time to think.

What happened next came from somewhere inside me, or somewhere beyond my physical body, or both, because I feel now they are one and the same.

My spiritual Self beyond my physical body activated in the most tangible way I had ever experienced. In previous spiritual experiences, I remained very much embodied. In this moment, I felt like 95% of my presence and the mode through which I was expressing was my Soul rather than my ego, or even my physical body, as it was so completely dense from the drug.

I experienced an energy like pure steel emerge through my being and expand outwards, creating an egg-like containment with an unbreakable barrier of protection.

I felt Cristian's energy shift. Giddiness and excitement turned to doubt in his eyes and a searching in his voice.

I felt immense power emanating from me. I could barely move, and it still took every ounce of me to speak, yet this impenetrable life-force energy beamed from me and throughout this steel egg encompassing me. I felt a wisening as well. Though the desperate voice of denial was still booming in me, I felt an inviolable, Herculean energy, as though an invisible shift had happened—a power dynamic that was never named was suddenly and irrevocably altered. Cristian exuded anxiousness, while my Soul exuded untouchable strength and clarity.

I was managing terror, the threat of physical collapse, and ongoing dialogue with the part of my brain that was determined to gaslight me out of seeing the reality that I was being violated by a man with an agenda.

This dialogue unveiled a layer of my subconscious. I had always been a strong woman who took risks to voice injustices and stand up for herself in high stakes, yet here I was facing the impending threat of rape while getting bludgeoned by a voice in my own head insisting I was crazy.

The stark contrast of this voice next to my own strong-willed nature made me realize the voice of humanity's wounded feminine programming was wired into my subconscious. This is the collective voice of generations of women dominated, abused, gaslit, and suppressed into cages of dulled expression and disempowerment.

While my body was undeniably responding to a toxic substance coerced into its bloodstream, this programming of playing the quiet "good girl," of internalizing the abuse of the traumatized masculine, was as alive inside me as my own heartbeat.

Sitting in the taxi, I had to constantly re-attune my awareness to my Soul's energy of impenetrable protection so as to maintain lucidity and fierce sovereignty. I had never felt so burdened by paradox, so intimately embodied in various aspects and dimensions of my being all in the same moment—a moment of the most extreme terror I had ever experienced.

At the core of my being, the message was clear. I may have been violated physically, a toxic substance put into my body against my will, but I was NOT going to allow myself to be violated any further.

We wound along the long, dark mountain road where only quick moments of cell service went away as soon as they came. I was intensely managing all the voices and dimensions inside me while attempting to discern a clear path of action to save myself from impending threat. I began texting a friend.

I yearned for a protective male presence. I typed the message, unsure if it would be sent in this disconnected high mountain pass. The voice of the suppressed feminine grew stronger again. A wave of embarrassment, of shame, rushed through my being.

It said, "*I can't tell him this is happening. This **isn't** happening, I'll look like such a fool. He'll scoff at me. My reputation will be ruined.*"

When I dropped out of that loud voice and into my body, I *knew* what I knew. Amidst deception, patriarchal programming, and overwhelm, the one thing I could absolutely anchor to was the felt sense in my body. Nothing and nobody, not even the voices in my head, can tell me I am not having this physical experience.

I broke through this relentless voice and sent the message. It took some time, every moment feeling like a year, but miraculously, it sent.

Cristian, watching me on my phone, spoke with a desperate quiver in his voice.

"Do you have service?"

The energy of steel expressing from my Soul, despite the immense physical heaviness and depth of fear I was experiencing, spoke for me.

"Yes," I said, with such lucidity and power it was like a knife cutting through the deception and violation he had enacted.

He was officially on the defense now.

We were coming close to the first stop in the Sacred Valley. I knew there would be an entrance with a big sign, street lights and people awaiting transportation. There would be life. I wouldn't be alone. I would be safe in the presence of onlookers.

Shockingly, I received a response from my friend at the same moment. He confirmed my path of action, "As soon as you get to Pisac, get the hell out of the car—fast."

I knew what I had to do. Cristian had fallen silent. The energy was draining from him and fueling me. I felt the power of my agency, my will to survive, cutting through the density in my body. I felt myself gathering into an energetic stance—the stance of the warrior, ready for battle, poising herself to look death in the face.

This energy was rising at the same pace as he was freezing, and at last, I saw the first sign signaling Pisac. It would be just minutes now before my call to action.

I was at the apex. I felt all the strength, will-force, and power of my Soul coming to climax. Simultaneously, the voice of the wounded feminine pleaded her story in equal measure; it was the light versus the dark within, the fear versus the immortality of consciousness.

It was the final hour—speak now or forever hold my peace.

The power of the programmed feminine voice was so strong, I had to use a massive sword of Spiritual resolve to pierce its age-old illusion and the grip it has had on humanity and the planet for thousands of years... and that's exactly what I did. My Soul prevailed and cut through the deception by speaking aloud.

"I am getting out of the car in Pisac."

My words, though at a normal volume, seemed to blare like the voice of the Goddess declaring her presence.

He seemed to crumble. Somehow, even though he had the power to lock the doors and enforce domination, he felt the power beyond my human self as it declared justice and sovereignty, and his falsity buckled.

Mere moments passed before we arrived, and as soon as he braked, I flung the door open. I acted faster than my mind could comprehend. I jumped out of the front seat and flew to the back door to throw my stuff to the street. He fumbled in the driver's seat, grabbing his phone and sending a voice message in Spanish that I couldn't fully understand, but heard him in a panicked voice say, "Give me a minute."

"*Was someone awaiting our arrival?*" I thought. As I threw the rest of the bags out of the trunk, he came to the back—panicked, confused, and wide-eyed.

"Did I do something? Did I *do* something?! What's wrong?!" He pleaded desperately. I grabbed my wallet, threw him some money, and stood on the side of the road with all of my things.

Chest heaving, adrenaline racing, my one sole focus was to get myself home immediately.

To my disbelief, he fumbled back to the car and drove off.

I made it home. I was stunned. *"Did that really just happen? Did I make all that up? What is real and what is illusion?"*

A wave of disgust overcame me. I cleaned the house with urgency, attempting to bring about cleanliness and a sense of control.

Before I went to bed, Cristian texted me... several texts in a row. No full sentences. I felt his anger in the flurry of impatient and impulsive words. The words were choppy, insinuating that nothing happened, and that I was crazy for acting the way I did. It was fueling the flames of the wounded feminine narrative—that *I* am the crazy one, that I can't believe what I feel in my own body because **HE must be right.**

When I awoke the next morning, he had deleted the flurry of volatile messages. Deleting the evidence. It helped soothe the voice of denial, which had already eased greatly during my sleep.

Yet, a fog of illusions remained like smoke and mirrors all around me. Having only taken one gulp of the drugged water bottle, a nebulous liminal state was created. Had I ingested more, it could have quickly caused my body to collapse. Having experienced taking drugs before, and being sensitive to subtle energies, I felt the effect of this substance as soon as it entered my bloodstream. Yet the subtlety made the incredibly loud voice of the suppressed feminine *so* confusing. It was like having an internalized abuser gaslight my own direct experience.

I was born, raised, and bathed in a society that utterly denies subtle energy. If you sense subtle energies, let alone name them and call out wrongs in their name, you're called mentally imbalanced, looked down upon or, like so many of our ancestors, demonized and murdered under the name "*Witch.*"

While I was in that taxi, I felt lifetimes of the collective feminine voice. I felt my own lineages and all the women who were told to sit down, shut up, and play the role of obedient, acquiescing, closed-lipped woman. The oppressed feminine was a volcano finally erupting after generations and lifetimes of suppression, all-encompassing in its unbridled expression.

Because of my work with somatic modalities and attuning to astrological transits, I knew I was personally in a rite-of-passage involving deep psychological crucibles, and was able to become present with myself on every level in the days following this traumatic event. I shook my body vigorously, sobbed in organic undulating waves of emotional release, wrote out my mind's overwhelm and inherent desire to comprehend the incomprehensible, hugged a pillow when I needed comfort, sat in spacious silence, and spoke to trusted kin.

The wisdom of astrology and understanding our sacred body intelligence through somatic study allowed me to step out of victim consciousness and into empowerment. I slowed down and became so present, minutes felt like hours—beyond space and time. It was psychedelic, like entering the realm of the heart, of the Soul, and experiencing how these non-physical aspects of ourselves heal in miraculous ways.

This was the first time I processed an acutely traumatic event in real-time, and the results astounded me. I had a directly embodied experience affirming that by having an awareness of the impact of traumatic overwhelm to the nervous system, and knowing tools and practices to meet that impact, we are capable of welcoming the arc of completion. When we make space for *all* parts of ourselves to express following a traumatic event, the body, emotions, mind, and Soul know how to rebalance our beings.

I ended up living in the Sacred Valley for three more years, enjoying a beautiful and magical life. I was never afraid to be in a taxi or in Peru.

The worst experience of my life alchemized into an essential truth that awakened in my very cells—we do not have to be warped into contracted versions of ourselves because of violations put upon us. I was no longer a child. I was an empowered adult woman who could alchemize anything life threw at her, even her deepest fears, turning toxicity into pure gold that awakened the Soul power within.

In the end, my Soul knowing told me this:

In response to an age-old patriarchal violation, I allowed the wisest, most expansive part of myself to be embodied into my physical form. She did not just speak for me, she spoke on behalf of generations of women and thousands of years of domination and violation of the feminine.

She said:

"THIS ENDS NOW."

She and my ancestors made thin air, my energetic space, turn into steel.

She made the impossible real and tangible—my incapacitated body stayed conscious against all rational definition of how an immobilizing drug impacts the body.

She, after thousands of years of being demonized and repressed, said:

"I AM HERE NOW."

Because I said **YES** to her arrival and gave her the reins.

About Cheyenne Marie Wright

I am an Astrologer, Soul Tender and Embodiment Midwife. I weave the ancient wisdom of astrology with somatics to activate and guide clients' expansion of their Soul-led life. Soul Embodiment Experiences intertwine sacred body intelligence with the astrological blueprint and timeline, threaded together by ritual, to support actualization of Soul callings.

Having developed my method through direct experience, I ignite others to follow their Soul's voice through transformational sessions, writing, and walking my talk. My own Soul Embodiment Journey was initiated through childhood experiences of poverty, a 3-year dark night of the Soul that sparked brutal yet beautiful spiritual awakenings, and living in Peru. These initiations kindled the actualization of living my dream as a traveling writer and philanthropic entrepreneur. From lived experience, and with fierce love, I guide those ready to expand into the next level of their Soul-led lives in co-creation with the celestial elders.

From 1:1 session packages to retreats in the Sacred Valley of Peru, adventure awaits in Soul Embodiment Experiences.

4% of revenue goes directly to initiatives that support Andean women, children and families.

Find me on Instagram @cheyenne.marie.wright
Website: www.cheyennemariewright.com

Scan QR code for my newsletter of astrological transmissions & the free creative mapping mini-workshop: *My Personal Map to Soul Embodiment—Weaving Astrology, Somatics & Ritual.*

SPIRITUAL COURAGE AND CONVICTION

Chapter 17

AM I GOING TO HELL?

Annette Jacobson

A shiver of fear runs through every cell of my body as I ask myself, "*Am I going to Hell?*"

I am standing in the church office... a dark, windowless room. The church itself is cold and damp, large and cavernous, and defined by sculpted stark gray concrete walls, high wood ceilings, and dingy brown carpeting. Although I am the church president and leader of the women's Bible study, I feel the loneliness and desperation of the journey to eternal damnation.

As I feel the burning terror of it, I hear my own voice. "Even if Christianity is not what I was taught, even if the Bible is not what I thought, the Divine ~ the Universe ~ God ~ there is still THAT, and I know in my being... THAT is love. Even in the shattering of my faith and beliefs, I am held by that love. I will not shatter with the rest."

I experience my own free fall into dark spaciousness. It is so unfamiliar, so uncomfortable. I do not know who I am without my faith. I am used to feeling full, to having a community and a book to go to that has the answers. Now the foundation of my entire lived experience is gone.

What happened? I was always a spiritual seeker, curious, wanting to experience life fully, deeply, meaningfully. I recall sitting in that dark church one Sunday while president. In the cold quietness, the congregation was reciting the Apostle's Creed together.

"I believe in God the Father," and I stopped.

"*NO!*" I screamed inside, "*I do not believe God is Father anymore, not in my heart, my head, or my spirit.*"

"And in Jesus Christ, his only son, our Lord."

"*No way ~ God's only son? And my Lord?*"

"Who was conceived by the Holy Ghost."

"*Just who is the 'Holy Ghost?' Who is this Spirit, anyway?*"

In my decades of being a Christian, I had read the Bible in its entirety twice, and studied the books in it numerous times, committing much of it to memory. And yes, I was finally admitting to questions I'd had for years. How could the Holy Spirit of God live *in* me, and yet I am still able to be me ~ Annette, a woman living on this planet? The Apostle Paul said, "It is not I who live, but Christ who lives in me." This never made any sense to me at all. How in the world was this supposed to happen, and yet I still am uniquely, beautifully created by God, by the Divine?

The seed of my courage split open and sprouted when I had the audacity to admit these things to myself. There were not only these questions, but others. How could fundamental, evangelical Christians teach that women were not to be leaders in the church? My blood boiled in anger as I considered the gifts women have: to lead, to guide, to do all the things men did, and it was all going to waste. They also taught, and truly believed, that homosexuality was a sin. My stomach turned with nausea just allowing myself to consider this. How could this be what they believed? I had friends who were gay. In my spirit and lived experience, I knew that they were some of the most amazing, loving, gifted friends I had. God is love ~ oh, wait, I'd heard their canned answer before, spoken with a saccharine sweetness and superiority: "Love the sinner, hate the sin."

From time to time during my years in Christianity, I would consider these questions, and I would be told by church leaders, "Look in the Bible. It's in the Bible." But that response was disconcerting, like a sliver that continued to hurt every time I touched it.

And then one day, the opportunity came to really ask the questions again. But this time it was different. This time I was open to hear different answers, *real* answers.

While I was president of my Lutheran church, the congregation of that cold, cavernous building was going through the process of deciding if we should become a "welcoming" congregation. In our liberal Lutheran synod, that would mean that we welcomed LGBTQ people openly and gladly ~ as equals to us all. This process involved discussions during the Sunday School time between church services. Even before we had gotten very far in the process, some members had already left to join other churches. They could not fathom even *considering* welcoming these folks: after all, wasn't the Bible clear that it's a sin to be that way? They conveniently overlooked our gay church organist.

For those of us who stayed, there was a booklet we received, to be read and discussed. It had two articles, each written by a different highly respected biblical scholar. One was conservative and wrote about how homosexuality was clearly a sin, citing scripture to back up that perspective. The other one was liberal, and using scripture, determined that homosexuality was clearly not a sin. I read these two articles very carefully. Up until that point in my life, from my early twenties into my fifties, I had based my spirituality, my mystical lived experience, on the Bible being the Truth ~ Divine words. Suddenly presented with the idea that there is no clear right or wrong in the interpretation of the Bible, my body responded like a lightning rod struck by a bolt of electricity. Resonating with the truth I had always held in my being, it split me open to consider all the questions and doubts I'd had for decades.

Where would I turn for answers? Synchronicity, the Universe, and the Divine provided abundantly.

Prior to a vacation, I was browsing in the local Barnes and Noble, looking for a book to bring along. I found myself in the spirituality section, where I came upon the memoir, *The Dance of the Dissident Daughter*, by Sue Monk Kidd. I began discovering history I had not known, foreshadowing my next few years of searching.

I also worked out at the Y regularly, with intelligent, creative, open individuals. On one particular day, I entered the machine room: it was bright and noisy, the air heavy with effort. I went over to the magazine stand and picked up the latest weekly periodical. I placed it in front of me as I stepped onto the elliptical machine, reading it while I moved my arms and legs. I opened the magazine straight to the book review section, and was surprised to discover some amazing authors and their books. There were authors like Elaine Pagels, a biblical scholar who wrote about the Gnostic Gospels, and Karen Armstrong, an expert on world religions who had also written spiritual memoirs. These books and others, like *The Alphabet Versus the Goddess* by Leonard Shlain, would play a role in opening my mind and spirit.

I finished my workout, grabbed my towel to wipe the sweat from my face, and put the magazine back. As I opened the door to the hallway, I ran into my spin instructor, Charlie, and commented, "Wow, I've just learned about an author named Karen Armstrong!"

Charlie replied, "She's great, isn't she? Which books have you read of hers?" The discussion that commenced with him for the next few minutes filled me with energy and joy, affirming that my current seeking and openness was indeed the path for me.

I entered the locker room and ran into another friend, Martha. She had her kickboard and fins in hand after completing a swimming workout. I'd learned she was a Methodist minister and had a congregation at one time, though now she had moved on to being a couples therapist. I told her about my questions and struggles.

"Annette, I don't believe all of the dogma that the church teaches, either." Wow! If I hadn't felt I had full permission to doubt and choose not to believe, I now did... and from a minister herself. She was a good friend who was supportive when I came to her with the latest book I was reading, or question I was considering, and she gave me the names of other authors to consider, one of them being Episcopalian minister John Shelby Spong.

The Y was surrounded by synchronicities. On my way home, with NPR tuned in on my car radio, I would listen to Krista Tippet's program, *Speaking of Faith*. She interviewed the theologian Bart Ehrman, and I was introduced to one of his books on how the Bible was created.

Slowly, I pieced together the historical facts of how Christianity came to be, and how the Bible was created. The more I read, the angrier I became. Though I had been indoctrinated into the Christian culture, I had never heard this history before. The facts pointed to politics, patriarchy, and power being at the foundation of the church and the Bible, and no one had ever bothered to teach me this. Learning about this cracked open the foundations of my faith, which had been built, Sunday after Sunday, within the culture of the church I was brought up in.

The church was another home for me as I was growing up. Bright sunshine streamed through the windows that lined the length of the sanctuary, which felt like a warm, happy hug of love on Sunday mornings. Many of my friends and classmates were there, along with my parents' friends. It was just two blocks away from one of my childhood homes, set on a corner and backing onto one of the lakes that the city was built around.

I enjoyed going to choir. I loved the music and singing, especially the alto harmony that created fullness and complexity with the other voices. The music touched my heart and spirit, giving me a safe place to feel and express myself.

I also went to sleepaway summer Bible camp in grade school, where rustic cabins faced a tree lined lake in northern Wisconsin. There were fun games and swimming, and young counselors who made me feel loved and safe as we played, ate, and sang around the campfire. I even had a crush on one of the high-school-aged counselors. I wrote him a letter after I got home, and bless his heart, he wrote back and put a sticker with love and hearts and flaming lips on the envelope! Such fun!

In junior high, I attended three years of confirmation classes on Saturdays, culminating in a ceremony to confirm my faith in 9th grade. There were tests from time to time, and I recall after one of the last exams, Pastor Olsen came up to me, smiling, and said, "There was a question on the exam ~ you may remember it. It asked if you should learn about your faith before confirmation or afterward. You were the only one who said 'Both.' Great answer!" What a nice pat on the back for me!

Because it felt so good to be in church, I began to read my Bible every night to recreate that experience. But my Revised Standard Version had thin, dry pages packed with tiny print, and though I tried to find that same warmth and joy, it was like eating sawdust.

I recall asking one of my classmates who also went to my church, "Do you read your Bible every night?" I hoped to find the secret to it coming to life.

But instead of discovering the secret, I was shocked when she screwed up her face and said, "Of course not!"

I thought everyone was curious about having a spiritual experience. Since I was raised Lutheran, going to church and reading the Bible were the avenues I knew about to deepen my experience. Despite her unexpected response, I continued on, always curious, but not getting much further.

College came, along with living in the high-rise cement block dorms at the University of Wisconsin. Freshman year was finishing up, and my friends and I were looking forward to the summer break. It was late afternoon when there was a knock at my dorm room door.

"I'm Mindy from Campus Crusade for Christ. It's a Christian organization on campus. Would you be interested in coming to a small group Bible study?"

Would I? It was what I had been waiting for! Soon I was going to a Bible study with a small group of college women, and eventually I began to go to the larger Tuesday night meetings. These were for the entire organization, with a lot of singing and sharing. I began to feel that wonderful combination of joy, safety, fun, and acceptance. My heart was touched by the music, and during the small group Bible study, with the help of the kind and loving leader, Laura, the words of the Bible finally came alive. My spirituality deepened and grew.

However, a piece of dogma within this culture began to whisper to me, getting louder and louder until, like a train whistle approaching from a distance, it roared in my soul, making a huge impact on my life. I was brought up believing that those who went to church and were baptized were Christians. But I was to learn that there was a different definition of being a Christian. That new definition would affect one of the most important relationships in my life.

This relationship began when I was 13 years old. Tom and I met on a band trip, crossing Lake Michigan on the ferry. His mother had made cowboy cookies for him to bring along, and he walked over, opened a coffee can filled with them and asked, "Would you like a cookie?" That resulted in my nickname, "Cookie." We were a couple on and off until I was 16, and then we became inseparable. I was Lutheran and he was Catholic, so we would attend each other's church services together throughout high school.

During my sophomore year in college, Campus Crusade for Christ introduced me to the dogma that challenged this important relationship. There was a verse from the Bible that kept ringing in my ears, along with others' interpretation of it. "Do not be unequally yoked with unbelievers" (2 Corinthians 6:14). I was told, "It doesn't mean just those who don't identify as Christian, you know. It means those who aren't 'born again' and have a personal relationship with Jesus, like you do." Try as I might, Tom was not interested in any of the new activities that I was involved in. I asked myself again and again, *"How can this relationship be wrong? It isn't what I was taught growing up. And besides, we love each other so much!"*

Time and time again, I considered breaking up with him, but it did not feel comfortable or true or right. My inner voice, my own wisdom, could not agree with it. But I had been taught *not* to trust my own inner voice. I was a sinner ~ after all, what did I know? So I thought, *"If breaking up is what needs to happen in order for me to continue on the spiritual path, I really need to consider it."* My authentic self ~ my soul ~ had a voice that was still small and easily overcome at the time. So, with great pain, heartbreak, and tears, I broke off my relationship with Tom.

However, I found it challenging to make the decision stick. For almost four years, I would initiate getting back together, only to break up again ~ like ripping a bandage off over and over again. But our love for each other was strong and deep. When Tom graduated with his master's degree and moved out east, I followed at his invitation. Despite the turmoil inside of me, for one of the first times in my life, my own heart and soul spoke... and I listened. We had a deep foundation of love, and a lot in common. He was an amazing, good man and our souls were saying *yes* to each other. We married on a sunny, hot summer day in upstate New York on a hilltop overlooking a tree lined bend in the Susquehanna River, surrounded by dear friends.

Over 20 years later, after I had left the church with my Christian faith shattered five years earlier, a bigger issue was revealed that had been hidden. I had allowed access to myself, my consciousness, and my soul to be controlled by the Christian culture, dogma, and structure of the church, without ever realizing it. Access to the person who I was had shattered along with it. I suddenly realized I didn't know myself AT ALL. What I liked, what I didn't like, what made me happy, what made me fulfilled ~ I didn't have a clue.

In the dark spaciousness, with the anger ebbing and the frustration of not knowing myself growing, I began exploring. I participated in a couple of sprint triathlons for fun, and became curious about the mind-body connection (What did that mean, anyway?). I started to take yoga classes, enjoying the movement, and I began to develop the skill of awareness.

I dove in further, discovering Steven Cope's books on yoga, *Yoga and the Quest for the True Self*, and *The Wisdom of Yoga*. I went on my very first yoga retreat to Costa Rica. The beauty of the retreat center was magical ~ nestled into steep hillsides, there were colorful plants surrounding every cottage, and the heavy air was filled with their sweet fragrance. The powerful yoga and amazing Ayurvedic and energetic body treatments, along with the support of friends, added to the impact of the experience.

At the yoga retreat, my heart opened up in a way I had never experienced before. As I was filled with a new, bright, colorful, tingling spaciousness... tears flowed.

"What spoke to the rose to break it open broke open my heart."

Those words of the Sufi poet Rumi rang through my entire being. I was broken open, vibrating in color and love, with a joy I hadn't known before.

Not surprisingly, I decided to go deeper into yoga and take yoga teacher training. I enjoyed learning an entirely new paradigm, discovering that here, too, in other sacred writings, was truth. However, over time, I began to observe in the yoga community the same dogmatic approach to philosophy that I had known in Christianity. "*So this can happen with any teaching, with any paradigm.*" This realization struck me deeply. I continued to explore, with newfound awareness of this pitfall.

As I found the strength to be courageous, I used my power to decide to explore something different, which radically changed my life.

I discovered there was a need to be open to different ideas, to have courage, strength, and awareness. When I feel that physical discomfort in my abdomen, it is my inner wisdom saying, "*Pay attention! Something's not right.*"

I discovered I could embrace my power. Yes, I can make a different choice ~ a choice to learn, explore, investigate, be curious about life; a choice to honor the still, quiet voice in my heart. That freedom to choose brings me much spaciousness and joy.

Embracing that freedom, I have explored yoga, feminine power, the entrepreneurial world, different sorts of spirituality and mysticism, mediumship, consciousness, quantum physics, the human potential movement, philanthropy, and more.

My exploration and discovery continue, and I expect they will never end.

In my entire being, I know that I am not going to hell. My husband is not going to hell. The gay church organist is not going to hell.

No one is going to hell.

As long as my body has breath, I am living a rich, expansive life. And when there is no more breath, I expect to continue on to a new amazing adventure.

ABOUT ANNETTE JACOBSON

There was a time when Annette Jacobson didn't know who she was ~ and everything changed when she remembered.

Challenges became the catalysts that guided her exploration of unfamiliar paradigms in her search for purpose and meaning. She found more than that ~ her own self, her birthright of joy, and the impact of living an authentic life. As a writer, artist, and published author, she now helps others do the same.

Annette is a vibrant, curious spirit who walks the threshold between deep inquiry and everyday wonder. Her supertaster's palate enjoys a lovingly prepared meal as much as her soul revels in a painted canvas or the discovery of travel. She finds inspiration in birdsong, bike rides, deep conversation, and the shared journey of awakening.

Visit www.annettejacobson.com or email her at annette@annettejacobson.com to receive your free gift: *"The Seeker's Library: Books for Your Spiritual Journey."*

Chapter 18

LIFE IN A BATTLEFIELD:
THE BIRTH OF STORY MEDICINE

Laura Joan Cornell, PhD

There are three battlefields that have lived inside me since the day I was born, and I believe they are very much alive in the wider United States today as well.

I carry these conflicts in my body, my family, and my spirit. My response to them has led me to develop what I now call *Story Medicine*.

THE CIVIL WAR

The most recent battlefield lives in the legacy of the United States Civil War: North versus South, a divide that still echoes in our politics—liberal versus conservative, red versus blue.

In my own family, I carry both sides within. On my grandmother's side, there's an old photo with a typeset name at the bottom: *Kentucky Veterans of the Confederate Army*. About 20 men stand shoulder to shoulder. Though my grandmother rarely spoke of it, I know that either her grandfather or great-uncle is pictured there.

On my grandfather's side, we have the discharge paperwork and detailed military records of an ancestor who fought for the Union. He survived malaria and a bayonet wound in Indiana, returning twice to the front before rising to officer and participating in the Union's final victory.

Yet the Civil War never truly ended. Its unfinished business still rages today in our politics. One side calls the other "racist," while the other labels their opposition "un-American." Some believe they stand for the Constitution; others, for progress and humanity. Each claims freedom and moral truth. Beneath it all, I feel an old wound—unhealed and inherited.

War trauma sows transgenerational violence, both physical and sexual. Outwardly, my family appeared pious—many of my ancestors converted to Christian Science around my grandparents' generation—but the violence simmered dangerously and unpredictably, never far from the surface.

I've heard stories of my grandfather's rage—how he could be cruel to his children, though by the time I knew him, he was gentle and sweet. If you met my father now, at eighty-eight, you might find him gentle too. But when I was young, he lost his temper many times on his children, on me. When I was just two, my mother had to pull me away from him after he "lost it" so severely that I was black and blue the next day. The scars of that trauma still live in every fiber of my body.

Now, as a facilitator of Family and Systemic Constellations, I've come to see how often we form cross-cultural relationships in an effort to heal ancestral and collective wounds. Descendants of people who fought on opposite sides of a war will often intermarry. Descendants of Holocaust survivors marry those of German heritage. Descendants of colonizers and the colonized find each other and create new families. Ancestral pieces that remain unresolved are passed to their children, and their children's children, in the form of unconscious shadows that influence us profoundly without our knowing.

THE INVASION OF EUROPEANS INTO THE AMERICAS

Continuing backward through time, the next battlefield is the invasion and pillage of these beautiful American continents—North and South—and their native peoples. European colonizers did not come with the consciousness of equality and sharing, but with domination. They were greedy; they gobbled up and "claimed" the land and often its peoples, breaking treaty after treaty and leaving deep scars.

These wounds live on in our debates over inter-American relations and how to manage borders, especially the U.S.–Mexico border.

The immigration debate today is painfully polarized. Accusations and political name-calling abound, but real dialogue is rare. We argue over what is compassionate or not, the costs of immigration, and border laws—but the deeper wound is rarely named: the centuries-long history of injustice.

I was born in Oakland, on Ohlone land. I grew up in southern Illinois, land of the Sioux, and later returned to the Ohlone and Miwok territories. Now I live in Arizona, home to the Apache, Yavapai, Hopi, and Paiute.

I have a past-life memory as a native woman in the heart of what is now the United States. Whether true or not, this resonance lives in me. I feel deeply connected to the land of the Americas. Biologically, I'm European American, but I feel a kinship with the native blood I believe I've carried before.

As a child, I found arrowheads in the cornfields behind my house. I roamed the native grasses along the bluffs of the Mississippi River. In my solitary hours, I sat under Illinois oaks—native trees—gathering acorns and mixing magic earth potions, feeling something ancient come alive in me.

This connection deepened in adulthood. I joined Shoshone elders in sweat lodges, protested underground nuclear weapons testing on their lands, and got arrested in the process. I met Guatemalan refugees in southern Mexico—Mayan families who spoke only their native Quiché. As an elementary school teacher in a Spanish bilingual classroom, I tried to soften the crossing for immigrant children and their families, bridging the immigration gap between North and South.

Latin America keeps calling me back. I speak Spanish fluently and feel my European mind soften when I cross the border into what I experience as warmth, music, and poetry. More than once, I fell in love in Latin America—relationships that felt like soul calls to bridge divides. Again, our soul's longing reaches toward unity through love and intimacy.

My husband and I were living in Mexico, stranded in San Miguel de Allende early in the pandemic. We then saw just how starkly the difference in financial means shaped what hunger looked like in the U.S. versus Mexico. While hunger became a concern in the U.S. months into the pandemic, in Mexico, food shelves in homes emptied within a week. We heard this from many people: adults skipped meals so their children could eat; taxi drivers used their small salaries to feed entire multi-generational households, plus their neighbors.

One morning, I leaned out our window to see a man who had walked miles with his mule and two sacks, calling out *"tierra"* (earth) as he sold humble dirt door to door, just to feed his family—a sight that has never left me.

I keep returning south. This spring, I visited Cuba and was stunned by the extent of U.S. influence and the fierce Cuban resilience. Once the "Pearl of the Antilles," Cuba fought off Spain only to fall under U.S. control in 1898. Decades later, Fidel Castro led another revolution to reclaim true Cuban sovereignty. The people are deeply proud of having won their independence. They told me, "We didn't expect Castro to be a communist. He said he wasn't." Still, they'll also tell you the system is broken. Life is incredibly hard; food and supplies are scarce. Yet the people's spirit is vibrant, and they often know more about the world than those of us living in the U.S.

These journeys keep teaching me the same truth: humanity is one. We all love, grieve, and dream. Latin America softened my intellect into something more whole and human. I cried for Cuba and for my violin teacher there. What lingers most is my deep yearning for cross-cultural kinship. This is personal to me. I've lived it in my lifespan and my lovespan.

THE BATTLE BETWEEN MEN AND WOMEN

The third battlefield is the war between men and women. This war runs deep, spanning millennia. It traces back to the conquest of peaceful goddess-worshiping cultures in southern Europe by northern horsemen, and to the story of Adam and Eve itself.

As I was writing this chapter, a client told me a story from her memoir: how she experienced orgasm during childbirth—her first orgasm came with her first child, her second with her second child. Only after those births could she orgasm with her husband.

She is not alone. I've heard this from other women too, and read that it's actually fairly common. I believe orgasm is a natural, healthy state for women—an embodied bliss that can even be a painkiller in childbirth. What a wonderful world it would be if we came to see this as the normal state of childbirth, and encouraged women to find sexual and spiritual ecstasy in labor, rather than pain and shame.

How different this is from the biblical story that cursed Eve to bear children in pain, robbing women of the potential ecstasy and clear empowerment of giving birth.

The war between men and women has many fronts, but perhaps its most brutal and explicit was the witch burnings of medieval Europe. I am heir to this, simply by being a woman, and I've heard many women say they feel their fear of owning their voice stems from those burning times.

As a teenager, I used to clash with my father at the dinner table over politics. One night we were arguing about nuclear war: I took the pacifist side, he the pro-nuclear stance. Later, my mother pulled me aside in the kitchen and said, "Laura, if you keep talking like that, no man will ever want to marry you."

My mother's fear for my future came from her own upbringing and from the same collective women's heritage of the burning times: the conviction that a "proper" woman keeps her opinions quiet. But I, Laura Joan Cornell, was never meant to be quiet.

Thankfully, my mother was wrong. I have been deeply loved by beautiful men (and two beautiful women)—my soft, sweet Jewish boyfriend in college; several kind Latino partners; and now my husband of eighteen years, Jim. Jim loves my voice. He delights when I pull out a scrap of paper on one of our hikes and say, "I have a few topics I'd like to discuss." He reads every word I write and offers his insights in return.

This war between men and women doesn't rage in my marriage, but I know it still lives in the wider world. Is it okay for women to have a voice? Do my clients feel safe using theirs? Do I feel safe using mine, especially now, in an increasingly fractured cultural landscape where one must tread so carefully?

Without realizing it, my mother planted a seed for my voice when she gave me my middle name, Jean. I asked her once why she chose it. She said she didn't know—she just liked how it sounded. I never liked it much myself, and later changed it to Joan. But symbolically, they are the same name. I am named, of course, after Joan of Arc—perhaps the most famous cross-dresser in history, a young woman who dressed as a man, heard divine voices, and helped the French throw the British off their land.

So, in a way, I'm living out the path of my namesake: telling stories, speaking truths, lifting my voice—so that other women may lift theirs as well.

STORIES AS MEDICINE FOR THE BATTLEFIELDS WITHIN

All of these traumas left me with a deep inner disquiet—a sense of being unsettled. In my adult life, I've had to work to find that place of inner peace while standing amid the legacy of physical and sexual violence, my place as a white European descendant living on American soil, and my journey as a woman.

How have I chosen to approach these battlefields? When facing family traumas, I found my voice and spoke my truth. I was able to stay connected to my parents through it all, though I know this is not always possible, or the best choice, for everyone.

One of the most powerful ways I have healed is by listening to and telling stories. I did this with my mother and sister, with friends, in therapy, and in countless women's circles over more than four decades.

As we reflect on the hard parts of our stories, we learn to befriend our pain and see how our wounds shaped our wisdom and strength. We honor our courage, soften resentment, and let go of grudges—not to excuse harm, but to free ourselves.

When we read another's story of turning pain into medicine, our world expands. I love learning from every woman in this circle—hearing memoirs of birth, aging, even orgasmic childbirth—yes, this too is sacred story medicine!

Most of all, I choose to use my voice and help other women stand in theirs.

MY LIFELONG LOVE AFFAIR WITH NONVIOLENCE

Stories, at their best, are bridges. They connect us with others across differences. And for me, the true power of storytelling is built on the same foundation as my commitment to nonviolence. Long before I ever led women's circles or published books, reading Mahatma Gandhi in high school awakened my lifelong love for yoga and my devotion to living gently in a turbulent world.

Nonviolence is at the heart of yoga, and I aspire to live it daily, however imperfectly. After Gandhi, I discovered the Quakers, famous pacifists who were the first religious group in the United States to oppose slavery as a unified body and who championed women's suffrage. Their deep respect for the inner voice helped me reclaim the truth of my own voice, the same voice my mother once feared would keep me from being loved.

Quakers believe there is a Light within each person and teach us to listen deeply inwardly for Its leadings. In Meeting for Worship, I would arrive restless and tangled inside. As time and silence settled my thoughts, my heart would loosen, and sometimes a message would rise to be spoken—or I'd be moved by words another Friend shared.

One of my most formative memories was witnessing my Quaker community discern whether to support same-sex marriage in the early 1990s, more than 20 years before it was legal in our state of California. Instead of debating, we held listening meetings in worship. One Friend remained opposed, but because we moved slowly and didn't force agreement, he eventually chose to stand aside, allowing us to move forward in unity. It taught me that true pacifism is not just the absence of conflict but the presence of patient, respectful listening.

CONFLICT RESOLUTION IN THE CLASSROOM

I was deeply shaped by the conflict resolution methods I learned as an elementary school teacher.

When I taught third and fourth grade in Concord, California, I discovered an approach called *Classroom Meetings*—circles where every child's voice is respected. Instead of the teacher imposing discipline for every playground scuffle or name-calling incident, the children, with guidance, learned to work things out in these mediated circles, much like restorative justice.

It took time for the kids to trust the process, but once they did, everything changed. Instead of playing judge for endless tattling and disputes, I watched them own up to their actions and suggest ways to make amends. Their solutions—like writing an apology letter—were often gentler and more easily accepted than punishments I might have imposed. The atmosphere grew calmer and kinder, and teaching became far more meaningful.

I remember Zach, a new student who disrupted this hard-won harmony. He was messy, clumsy, and constantly in others' space. The class was exasperated, but instead of isolating him, we brought it to the circle again and again. For two months, nothing changed—Zach couldn't acknowledge his behavior, and the kids were ready to give up. But I persisted.

One day, we had a turning-point circle. I asked each student to speak directly to Zach about how his actions affected them, without blame or cruelty. He was stunned. From that day on, he tried to change, and the class had more compassion for him, too. Friendship and cooperation returned, and the whole dynamic shifted.

Years later, a former student found me at a Pride Parade. He thanked me for that year, saying he'd felt "different" and teased, but our meetings made him feel safe and seen. I didn't even remember the details, but he did.

Those classroom circles taught me what Quaker Meeting had already shown me: conflicts resolve when people feel heard. Children want fairness and kindness, just like adults.

HOW HEARTFULNESS MEDITATION HAS SHAPED ME

In 2014, as I entered menopause and struggled with insomnia, I discovered Heartfulness Meditation. Feeling unglued and exhausted, meditation became my lifeline—a way to reconnect with my center and deepest self.

Heartfulness teaches us to quiet the mind, rest in the heart, and receive a subtle energy transmission from our divine guides that nourishes and expands our soul's journey.

When I was first introduced to this practice, I hesitated on learning it was led by a male guru. After years of rejecting patriarchal spiritual systems, I was cautious. But I decided not to say no until after I prayed about it.

Once home, I sat down to close my eyes and immediately received a clear message: "You will always be Divine Feminine.

You can never *not* be Divine Feminine. This practice will be good for you."

And with that, I scheduled my first sittings with a trainer and began practicing. Though I'd meditated before, this was the first time I felt truly capable on my own.

Years earlier in India, I'd visited the ashram of Sri Aurobindo and The Mother, where I felt her presence and heard, "I will help you." In my early Heartfulness sittings with a trainer, I felt her again, as if she were handing my spiritual progress over to new guides.

Heartfulness became home. The women in my local ashram, all born in India, took me under their wing and welcomed me as a sister. I trained for a half marathon with my new friends; we laughed and I enjoyed getting to know their children. It was a rich cross-cultural experience, as my husband and I were the only "American Americans" (as my friends called us) among the 200+ people at the regular Sunday Satsangs.

Before Heartfulness, I had studied Nonviolent Communication with Marshall Rosenberg, learning to become more aware of judgments and to avoid "enemy images." His giraffe puppet (representing the land mammal with the largest heart) symbolized the big-hearted perspective needed for true nonviolence. Heartfulness later wove these principles into Heartful Communication, a gentle, heart-centered way of speaking and listening that aligns beautifully with my path.

HOW I MANAGE THE NEWS & CONFLICT TODAY

In the face of increasing political divisiveness, I've developed a new habit: listening to news from *both* sides. As chaotic as that can feel, it helps me see the patterns more clearly—especially the name-calling and subtle (or not-so-subtle) put-downs that each side flings at the other.

When I previously watched or read only one side, I would unconsciously absorb its worldview and stop noticing its biases. Reading across the divide has become part of my spiritual practice. Of course, I still hold my own opinions—but I aim to hold them with awareness.

A PATH, NOT A DESTINATION: MY PHILOSOPHY OF NONVIOLENCE

While the Quakers helped me untangle my heart through communal listening, Heartfulness grounds me in my daily personal practice. I also practice Family and Systemic Constellations, bringing my shadows—when they rear their heads—to trusted guides. All of these help me to move in the direction of living nonviolence.

This is a path I walk daily, with humility and hoping to meet the world with a little more love each day.

My philosophy is simple but not easy:

First, *patience and compassion*—for myself and others. Violations run deep in our collective histories; being gentle with ourselves is essential.

Second, *radical respect*. No matter how strongly we disagree, I believe in allowing differences to exist.

Third, *honest self-inquiry*. Nonviolence starts within. I watch triggers, examine shadows, and listen before speaking.

Fourth, *careful speech*. In Nonviolent Communication, I learned to recognize and avoid "enemy images"—those words and phrases that dehumanize and divide. Put in simple fourth-grade language: no put-downs.

Finally, *stories*. Stories build bridges where opinions build walls. Stories remind us that, underneath our politics and pain, we are all startlingly alike. We all love. We all grieve. We all yearn and bleed and dream. We all carry shadows. When we truly listen to another's story—especially someone different from us—our heart softens, and our humanity expands.

I continue my work with stories today as a coach for new authors. Every collaborative book I compile is a deep and living circle. The women read and uplift each other's chapters. I read them. Our editor, Hyla, reads them. Together we deepen trust and see each other more fully. We expand our shared humanity.

Writing your story is one of the most profound ways to clarify, honor, and fully claim your experience. I love receiving, witnessing, and mirroring back these stories in a Soul Read for each author's medicine. It is an honor to amplify their wisdom through publishing, to celebrate each storyteller in our book launch parties, and to share wisdom in my telesummits with peers around the world.

Getting to know people across divides—different cultures, languages, and politics—is a spiritual practice, my rebellion against the war zones around us. Peace grows one conversation, one story, one heart at a time.

May I keep walking this path.

May my voice serve the divine current.

May my life invite others to do the same.

ABOUT LAURA JOAN CORNELL, PHD

Laura Joan Cornell, PhD (Yogeshwari) is a three-time best-selling author, Divine Feminine Yogini, and sacred writing mentor. She is the founder of Divine Feminine Yoga, through which she has directed nine online conferences empowering women's voices, and where she offers coaching, retreats, online courses, and leadership training for women worldwide.

Laura is author of the book *Moon Salutations: Women's Journey Through Yoga to Healing, Power, and Peace*. In previous work as Founder of the Green Yoga Association, Laura spurred a national movement towards Green Yoga studios, produced two major conferences on yoga and ecology, and sold 10,000 non-toxic yoga mats from her living room. She has been featured in Yoga Journal, Natural Health, Yogi Times, LA Yoga, and Common Ground magazines.

Laura lives with her husband and goldendoodle in beautiful Sedona, Arizona, where she enjoys hiking, gardening, playing violin, and pickleball. This is her third anthology of sacred feminine stories.

www.DivineFeminineYoga.com
www.MoonSalutations.com

Epilogue:
From Stars to Soil ~ Remembering Fifteen

Susun Weed,
Wise Woman Herbalist

At fifteen, I thought I belonged to the stars.
I didn't know that life would lead me back down, into the soft,
pulsing body of the earth —
where green blessings would root and grow.
This is the story of how it began.

This year is devoted to renewing old friendships.
What better old friend to embrace than my younger self?

Yesterday I received a cache of high school yearbook photos.
Single photos.
Group photos.
High school photos.

I remember those mean girls.
Their faces still unnerve me.
Haven't thought of them in sixty years.
But there they are.
Their viciousness echoes down the hallways of my memory.
And I am grateful that there was no social media available to them.

I remember the nice girls too.
Friendships that have been in my memory all these decades.
Smiles still lingering in my heart.

I remember teasing my hair.
Begging for lipstick.
And hating high school.
Loathing high school.

I spent most of my chemistry class complaining to Phoebe McAfee.
She wasn't in the photos, alas.
Where are you Phoebe?

My bestie—Adrienne Oxley—is in one photo.
I think of her so often.
She married PFC Cox while I was at UCLA.
That would have been 1963.
Haven't heard from her since.

Where are you my best friend?
How has your life been?
Did you have children?
Are you happy?
Are you content?
What moves you?

Phoebe listened to my heated diatribe about
the uselessness of high school.
Day after day.
Chemistry class after chemistry class.
At last, she challenged me:
"Take the SATs and go to college." I was astonished.
Amazed.
Gob smacked.
The goddess told me to stop bitching and start acting.

Unbreakable Spirit

Damn good advice.
Anytime.
So I did.

This pretty girl followed her friend's advice.
Took the tests.
Went to college.
With her sights set on the stars.
The actual stars.

I'd been a member of the Texas Astronomical Society
since I was twelve.
Even had a telescope of my own which I hauled everywhere.
Yup, I took it to summer camp.
What supportive parents.
Gratitude.

I applied to MIT.
They accepted me.
With a major in math.
And a focus on artificial intelligence.
(As an Aquarius I see the future first.
That's useful.)

But MIT said my chemistry was weak.
(LOL)
I had to take a summer chemistry class if I wanted to go to MIT.

With the stunning clarity and wisdom of my sixteen years,
I decided that I would never need chemistry,
That I wanted to enjoy my last summer at home,
And that my second choice — UCLA — would be just fine.

UCLA, unlike MIT, is a liberal arts college.
At MIT, I would have been allowed to continue to narrow my vision.

Math, advanced calculus, logic systems, statistics, physics.
My mind: laser-focused and far, far, far away.
In the stars.
Beyond the numbers.
Pure research.

At UCLA, I was required to broaden my focus:
Psychology, literature, drama, languages, sociology, art history,
archeology, paleontology, anatomy, biology.
People, places, stories.
A stew of new.
Shaking me up.

Bringing me, ultimately, down to earth.
Into nature.
And back to my body.

In beauty.
As a giveaway dance.
One with the earth.
Surrounded by green blessings.
Tingling with joy.

ABOUT SUSUN S. WEED
WISE WOMAN HERBALIST

Susun S. Weed is a pioneering voice in herbal medicine and natural approaches to women's health. Author of the best-selling Wise Woman series—including *New Menopausal Years*, *Breast Cancer? Breast Health!* and *Down There: Sexual and Reproductive Health the Wise Woman Way*—Susun has been a fierce advocate for holistic healing for over 45 years.

Her work is recommended by renowned experts like Dr. Christiane Northrup and herbalist Rosemary Gladstar. An outspoken critic of hormone replacement therapy long before its risks were widely acknowledged, Susun champions integrative medicine that empowers women. Her teachings span herbalism, nutrition, ethnobotany, and the psychology of healing. She has been featured on NPR, CNN, NBC, and in major publications such as *Natural Health* and *Woman's Day*.

Susun leads the Wise Woman Center in Woodstock, NY, where she trains herbal apprentices, teaches online, and hosts prominent spiritual teachers. She also mentors over 1,400 students through her correspondence courses and publishes a monthly newsletter.

Learn more at www.susunweed.com.

ACKNOWLEDGEMENTS

I want to express my sincere gratitude to all the teachers who guided me in excavating and trusting my stories. I am especially grateful to Caroline Foster at the California Institute of Integral Studies (CIIS), my first writing instructor there. The "Organic Inquiry" research method I studied at CIIS profoundly shaped my thinking, teaching me the power of interviews and the transformative potential of personal narratives. Thank you to Tom Bird for illuminating the power of immersive writing and the importance of finding flow.

I am deeply grateful to Hyla Hitchcox, who served as our proofreader, copy editor, line editor, and chief cheerleader. Your friendly encouragement and insightful suggestions consistently improved the clarity of our writing. You made the entire process more enjoyable and helped me think through important questions of content and intent.

To Wendy Willtrout, thank you for your tireless efforts as our "herder of cats," expertly gathering author photos and chapter versions, ensuring all materials reached publication, and patiently answering countless questions from the authors. This project would not have been possible without you!

My deepest appreciation goes to the team at Spotlight Publishing House. To Becky Norwood, thank you for your skillful management of the layout, cover design, final publishing details, and the countless other elements involved in marketing and promoting this book. Your grace and professionalism shone through every interaction with me and the co-authors.

To the authors, thank you for sharing so generously of yourselves. Your vulnerability, strength, and courage in telling these stories have been a profound gift to our Sacred Author Incubator. I know each of you has grown, not only by telling your own story but also through sharing this journey and supporting one another in community. Your stories will benefit many women and serve as a powerful healing force far beyond our circle. My prayer is that you receive every blessing you desire from this generous act of courage.

My heartfelt thanks to my husband, who read every word of my chapter and listened patiently to my dreams and reflections as I explored the meaning of this project and my contribution to it. Your unwavering encouragement—during this and every writing journey—along with the love and support you and our pup Millie provide, create the nurturing home and writing environment that make all of this possible.

Finally, I offer my deepest gratitude to Great Mother Spirit, the loving, wise presence I feel in every breath and daily meditation. I experience your physical presence in this beautiful Earth, with which I am privileged to commune daily amidst the red rocks of Sedona. You hold and carry me always.

About the Cover Artist

Aimee Tomczak, MA, LMFT, is an Artist, Psychotherapist, Intentional Creativity Coach and Painting Instructor. Her colorful & soulful paintings begin with an intention and layered process inviting mystical guidance to reveal faces of the feminine and rhythms of nature through color and pattern.

Her cover art painting, "Spiral Woman," reveals a wise feminine presence unleashing her power through the spiral path of courage and transformation. This painting symbolizes each author's awakening into her full divine power by sharing her courageous story.

Aimee leads popular "Art as Medicine" workshops both online and in-person at Fulton Crossing Gallery in California. She is passionate about guiding people to rediscover and claim their joy, power and inner knowing through creative expression.

Get Aimee's free gift, "Claim Your Creative Space," a 10-minute guided meditation here: https://mailchi.mp/7b5c0f82c0c9/ylgfnz1ybp.

Learn about Aimee's online workshops and in-person offerings at www.aimeetomczak.com.

View her Artwork, including originals, prints, and merchandise at: www.aimeetomczakart.com.

Contact Aimee at: Beloved3me3@gmail.com.

About Divine Feminine Yoga and Ananda Press

Divine Feminine Yoga was founded to help women heal ~ body, mind, and soul ~ so we can reach out to heal the planet.

Ananda Press features voices of wisdom in conscious conversation. Learn from soulful women who celebrate the Divine Feminine and Her transforming presence in today's world.

We offer:

- Global online conferences to inspire, uplift, and connect you with other lightworkers.
- Sacred writing immersions, courses, and mentoring.
- Story Medicine workshops and events.
- Retreats ~ both online and in-person in beautiful Sedona, Arizona.
- The opportunity to be featured in our books and online conferences.

Please join us to connect with like-minded women and expand and empower your voice.

Learn more and stay in touch:
DivineFeminineYoga.com
100 Sedona Street
Sedona, AZ 86351
888-423-8843

Also by Laura Joan Cornell, PhD

Moon Salutations:

Women's Journey Through Yoga to Healing, Power, and Peace

"Revelatory, insightful, fascinating, and beautiful. A must read for those women who practice yoga as well as those who don't." *Judith Hanson Lasater, PhD*, Author of *Restore and Rebalance*

"Laura has given us a great gift through the birthing of Moon Salutations!" *Nischala Joy Devi*, Author of *The Secret Power of Yoga*

"A wise, full moon of a book." *Amy Weintraub*, Author of *Yoga for Depression*

Available on Amazon and through Ingram Spark.

Claim your free Moon Salutations mini-course: www.MoonSalutations.com

The Flow Formula

Write Your Book with Ease

Get unstuck, find your rhythm, and finally finish your book.

You have a book inside you ~ waiting to be written. But if you've ever struggled with **writer's block, self-doubt, or overwhelm**, you're not alone.

The Flow Formula offers a **proven, intuitive method** to help you **tap into your creativity, trust your voice, and bring your book to life** ~ without the stress.

Inside, you'll discover:

- ❧ **3 simple steps to move from stuck to flow** ~ so you stop overthinking and start writing with confidence.

- ❧ **The 5 biggest mistakes that hold writers back** ~ and how to avoid them.

- ❧ **How to structure your book naturally** ~ so even complex ideas come together with ease.

- ❧ **The #1 myth that keeps new authors stuck** ~ and the shift that will finally help you finish your book this year!

Your book is ready. **Are you?**

Download your free guide now:
TheFlowFormula.How

www.ingramcontent.com/pod-product-compliance
Lightning Source LLC
Chambersburg PA
CBHW071656160426
43195CB00012B/1484